The LAW and CHRISTIAN ETHICS

A SERIES OF LECTURES ON ETHICAL ISSUES FACING SOCIETY TODAY

Published on behalf of
The CHURCH of SCOTLAND
BOARD of SOCIAL RESPONSIBILITY
in conjunction with
The Centre for Theology and Public Issues,
University of Edinburgh

by SAINT ANDREW PRESS

First published in 2001 by
SAINT ANDREW PRESS
121 George Street
Edinburgh
EH2 4YN

ISBN 0 86153 310 0

British Library Cataloguing in Publication Data
A catalogue record for this book is available from the British Library.

Typeset by McColl Productions, 61a North Castle Street, Edinburgh EH2 3LJ

Printed and bound by Bell & Bain Ltd., Glasgow.

Series editor: Hugh Brown
Design concept: Mark Blackadder
Photographs: Hugh Brown and Ian Baillie

Contents

Foreword

The Church of Scotland Board of Social Responsibility thought that the beginning of a new century was an appropriate moment to question traditional values and seek fresh insight and understanding. Therefore we decided to explore the far-reaching issue of 'The Law and Christian Ethics', and entered into partnership with the Centre for Theology and Public Issues. Together we decided to narrow the context to manageable proportions by examining through public lecture and debate six specific areas relating to the subject.

In an increasingly secularised society, legislation and public policy are largely determined by the prevailing spirit of the age rather than by the Judeo-Christian foundation embraced by our forebears. In a pluralistic society, the Christian world-view can often be totally discounted, and therefore there is a need to investigate whether there is any common ground between Christian and secular perceptions and whether the Christian faith now has any opportunity to influence forthcoming legislation.

Each chapter reflects the theology, philosophy and understanding of its author rather than any views which may be espoused by the Board or by the CTPI. We believe that these varied and stimulating lectures, delivered by individuals who are experts in their field, offer a valuable and challenging exploration of the relationship between Christian ethics and the law. Our hope is that this publication may prove a useful tool for those who are committed to being salt and light in our society, wrestling with the interface of faith and law.

There can be no more appropriate moment for the publication of such material than now, when many in our newly devolved Scotland seek to contribute as change-makers and moulders of developing legislation.

Ann Allen
Convener,
Board of Social Responsibility

1
The Law and Christian Ethics: Yesterday and Today

Lord Mackay of Clashfern

Lord Mackay of Clashfern and Ann Allen (chair)

I am honoured to be invited to give the first lecture in this series but I also believe it to be a heavy responsibility. The subject matter of this course of lectures is highly important today and I intend to approach it in a relatively simple but direct manner since I believe many people who would not regard themselves as scholars in any sense, and I reckon myself in that number, are concerned to know the principles that should regulate their attitude as well as the attitude of the Church to the law today.

I start with a short account of my own belief as to Christianity and the place of ethics within it. I believe that God is the creator of this world and of the human family. I believe that He has revealed Himself in the Holy Scriptures and particularly by the coming into this world of Jesus Christ who is God the Son, who was born of the Virgin Mary, who taught publicly for three years, was crucified, rose from the dead and after forty days ascended to Heaven where He is exalted a Prince and a Saviour and that he will return to judge the world at the last day. He has told us Himself that the Word which He has spoken will be the criterion of judgement on that day. When He left this world our Lord promised the gift of the Holy Spirit and He is working in the world still.

Since it is the Word of Jesus which is to be the standard in the final judgement it follows that it is by that Word that our lives should be regulated.

In the New Testament Jesus directs us in this connection, particularly to the Ten Commandments and to that marvellous summary of the Ten Commandments in the two, namely, 'To love The Lord our God with all our heart, with all our soul, with all our strength and with all our mind', and the second 'To love our neighbour as ourselves'. As Jesus said, 'On these two commandments hang all the law and the prophets'. So Christian ethics in its most succinct, general and clear form consists in these two commandments.

It is immediately noteworthy that these two commandments direct attention to the internal attitude. They are not in the first instance prescriptive of external behaviour and they must be taken along with the declaration that man looks on the outward appearance, whereas the Lord looks on the heart. And again, this point is beautifully and effectively made in Chapter 13 of Paul's first letter to the Corinthians in which he points out that good works and indeed the highest form of self-sacrifice is useless from the perspective of Christian ethics if love or charity is absent.

On the other hand, this love in action in the human heart will show itself in the way the person in whose heart it operates conducts himself. And, therefore, we have given to us the Ten Commandments as the principal headings of Christian ethics: the first four being concerned primarily with our duty to God, the latter six with our duty to our neighbours and so far as these regulate external activity they are the basis of a Christian moral code. As I have indicated, however, it would be a mistake to regard their external aspects and the observance of these aspects as a sufficient observance of the Christian moral code without regard to the attitudes of mind and heart from which these external observances spring.

I understand the New Testament to set these standards out as the standards for all people, not just for those who become disciples of Jesus Christ. As I mentioned, the Bible teaches us that God is the creator of the human family and, therefore, has a right to set standards for the behaviour of human beings. In the Shorter Catechism which was approved by the General Assembly of the Church of Scotland at Edinburgh on 28 July 1648 to be a directory for catechising such as are of weaker capacity, the first question is: 'What is the chief end of man?' and the answer: 'Man's chief end is to glorify God and to enjoy him forever'. It goes on to point out that the Word of God contained in the Scriptures is the only rule to direct us how we may glorify and enjoy Him and that the principal teaching of the Scriptures is what man is to believe about God and what duty God requires of man. On this basis I think it can be said, as I have often heard it said, that the Commandments which God has given us in his Word are, at least to some extent, like the maker's instructions and that they are intended to promote the happiness of each individual and of the community of human beings at large. There are many places in the Scripture in which misery is associated with breaching God's Commandments although we are cautioned most carefully against inferring from disasters falling upon particular individuals that they have been guilty of particular breaches of these Commandments. It is in the ultimate judgement rather than in any provisional judgement based upon contemporary occurrences that the results of disobedience will be assessed.

It is also to be noted that there is an essential unity about the obligations that God places upon mankind that makes it inadequate to speak of discrete Commandments or obligations as if they were separate one from another. If essentially the moral obligation is to love God and one's neighbour that will be broken by any failure to do so.

No one faced with this standard and looking back on his or her own life can claim not to have breached God's requirements. However much we might wish to turn back the clock, once we have breached the Commandments we cannot repair that breach although we may seek to avoid a repetition for the future. It is against this background that the Christian Gospel proclaims the sacrifice of Christ and his exaltation to God's right hand as a Prince and a Saviour to give repentance and forgiveness of sins. To thosewho have, by God's grace, come to receive the Lord Jesus Christ as their Saviour from sin, a new motivation of love is introduced. Those who have known forgiveness of their sins have a new and strong motivation to love the One through whose sacrifice that forgiveness came. This love also generates a desire to be free from sinning – what Thomas Chalmers referred to as: 'The expulsive power of a new affection'.

If you are with me so far it will be obvious that Christian ethics go far deeper than mere observance externally of rules with a sanction that if these rules are breached, punishment will follow.

I turn now to the law by which I would understand primarily the law of our

3

own country, Scotland. Although Scotland has been, since 1603, part of a United Kingdom with England and from 1707 until last year had a legislature in common with it, the law in Scotland remains; and since the creation of the Scottish Parliament in 1999 this is reinforced, distinct from the law applying in England and Wales. The law of Scotland is derived from the ancient customs, from decisions of the courts and enactments of the legislature. Prior to 1707 these enactments were of the Scottish legislature. The law which pre-dates the modern decisions of the courts was formulated in a reasonably complete and systematic way by our great institutional writers Lord Stair, Lord Bankton, Erskine and Bell in the general law and in the particular area of criminal law, Hume and Alison. These which are regarded in Scotland as of high authority take account of decisions of the courts made when these authorities were written, and insofar as there was no act of Parliament or relevant decision covering a question, were derived from a consideration of the older customs of Scotland or by reference to other authoritative works, and from time to time these included the Scriptures.

It is a general feature of parliaments that they can undo or alter enactments of their predecessors unless there is some special reason which prevents this. In countries with written constitutions parliament may not alter the provision of the constitution without some special procedure, possibly a referendum or a particular size of majority. Another reason which is very relevant today is where this country is party to an international convention in respect of which Parliament cannot properly introduce amendments in this country without the appropriate international procedure being invoked. In addition, acts of the Scottish Parliament before 1707 may be impliedly repealed by falling into desuetude. It is not sufficient that an act is an old one for this to occur, it requires the absence of any reported case in recent times in which the act has been given effect to, that there is evidence that it has long been disregarded in practice or that its provisions are out of accord with modern conditions.

I mentioned international conventions and there are two particularly important general treaties which have a profound effect on Scots law. The first of these is the Treaty of Rome which is the foundation treaty of the European Community, or as it is now, the European Union, with the various treaties modifying it which have effect in the United Kingdom by virtue of the European Communities Act 1972 and the statutes which have followed it in consequence of treaties amending the original treaty ratified since 1972. These which I will refer to together as the Treaty of the European Union provide that the legislative authorities of the Union can enact measures which are binding in the United Kingdom, either when they have the force of law in the European Union in which case they are said to have direct effect or by imposing an obligation which has the force of law on the United Kingdom to enact legislation in conformity with the measure. The courts of the United Kingdom, including those of Scotland, are obliged to give effect to such laws enacted under the treaty.

I believe the true theory of this position is that the United Kingdom Parliament has given the effect of law in the United Kingdom to those measures enacted by the legislative authorities of the European Union which are authorised under the Treaty of the European Union. If Parliament chose to repeal the act of 1972 and its successors the European legislation would no longer have the force of law in this country.

The second special situation arising from an international treaty or convention to which I wish to refer is the European Convention on Human Rights and Fundamental Freedoms which in terms of the Scotland Act has substantial effect in Scotland on the institutions of government in Scotland. It will apply to the rest of the United Kingdom in 2000, I understand. From the point of view of this lecture, this is a matter of considerable importance. Just as with the Treaty of the European Union it has the effect that institutions outside of this country can make decisions which have a profound effect on our law but this Convention has a more direct relationship with ethical matters than the other which, although it does have ethical repercussions, is primarily directed at regulating trade and commerce in the European Union and matters connected therewith. Under the Scottish Act and the Human Rights Act 1998 the terms of substantially the whole of the Convention become part of the law of the United Kingdom with the courts of this country adjudicating on these matters. Hitherto that Convention operated as an international treaty binding the United Kingdom as a Sovereign State to comply with its terms. Although originally conceived as a treaty between states it also made possible, for those states which were willing to grant it, a right of individual petition by citizens of that state to the judicial authorities in Strasbourg. Decisions by those authorities, whether the jurisdiction was invoked by a state or an individual citizen, were and are binding on the United Kingdom as a state. The effect of the recent legislation is, as my successor as Lord Chancellor put it, to bring home that jurisdiction in the sense that the courts of the United Kingdom can give effect to the provisions of the Convention without the parties desiring that effect having to go to Strasbourg to get it. On the other hand, it does not bring the jurisdiction home completely in the sense that a citizen disappointed with the judgement of the courts in this country could apply to the judicial authorities in Strasbourg for a different decision. This Convention is expressed as conferring rights on citizens in very general terms and those terms have been the subject of a great number of judicial decisions by the Court of Human Rights in Strasbourg which consists of judges from all the nations who are bound by the Convention.

There are, of course, a great number of other international conventions binding on the United Kingdom which have effect in our law, normally by being scheduled to an act of Parliament which enacts the terms of the relevant convention as part of the law of the United Kingdom. Examples occur in the carriage by air and carriage by sea.

I should also mention that a great deal of our law at the present time consists in subordinate legislation, that is to say legislation not made by Parliament itself but made by some body authorised to do so within limits which Parliament has set.

I come now to the relationship between the law of the land and Christian ethics as I have sought to explain these terms.

In the background paper to this series of lectures it is stated that: 'There is a recognition that our laws and institutions appear to be less related to Judeo-Christian traditions than in the past'. Let me take some illustrations. Basically, the Sixth, Eighth and Ninth Commandments are and always have been part of our criminal law. Indeed the Scottish criminal law has depended on the principles in these Commandments without much statutory elaboration. In contrast with the position in England where there are detailed statutory provisions dealing, for example, with theft and with offences against the person, the Scottish judges have been left by Parliament to apply the principles of these Commandments without significant interference.

It would be difficult to envisage a law against coveting as part of the secular law. The law relating to adultery in Scotland changed at the time of the Reformation. The Ecclesiastical Courts did not dissolve marriages although they did upon certain grounds pronounce Orders of Separation, and although this relieved the innocent spouse from the necessity of further conjugal cohabitation the marital bond was not severed and it would have been bigamy for one of the spouses to contract a second marriage during the lifetime of the other. But since 24 August 1560 the courts have been entitled to dissolve marriages on the ground of the adultery of either the husband or wife and by the Act 1573, Chapter 55, the Scottish Parliament introduced to the law of Scotland the possibility of divorce for desertion, while cruelty remained a matter for judicial separation until the passing of the Divorce (Scotland) Act 1938.

So far as the Fifth Commandment is concerned the law of Scotland creates financial obligations between parents and children who are both in life as well as conferring, for example, on children's rights in succession to their parent which the parent cannot by will defeat. These could be regarded as illustrations of the application of the Fifth Commandment which still subsists in our law. A law against blasphemy also exists but so far as legislation concerning Sabbath Observance is concerned it has all been either repealed expressly or has fallen into desuetude. Legislation relevant to wider aspects of morality has changed over recent years, for example, in relation to homosexual acts between consenting males of full age.

In the civil law one of the great developments in the later part of the last century was in the law of negligence, and the leading case which has been a leading case not only for Scotland but for the whole of the United Kingdom and for the Commonwealth has been the decision in *Donoghue* v. *Stevenson*. Incidentally, I want to mention that, in that case, the pursuer, Mrs Donoghue, was able to reach the House of Lords as the appellant by using the provisions for poor people which have long been a feature of the arrangements in Scotland under which those of limited resource were entitled to obtain representation, often of the highest quality, without having to pay for it and with protection against awards of expenses. This is surely an illustration of the Christian ethics of the legal profession in Scotland which has perhaps been obscured by recent criticism of the profession in relation to the statutory Legal Aid Scheme. However, the main point was that Mrs Donoghue went into a cafe in Paisley with a friend who ordered for her ice-cream and ginger beer. The ginger beer which was provided in compliance with the order was manufactured by the defender Stevenson. The bottle was made of dark opaque glass and Mrs Donoghue and her friend had no reason to suspect that the bottle contained anything else than the aerated water, some of which the friend poured into a tumbler. Mrs Donoghue drank some of the contents of the tumbler. Her friend then lifted the ginger beer bottle and was pouring out the remainder of its contents when a snail which had been in the bottle and was in a state of decomposition floated out of the bottle. In consequence of the nauseating sight of the snail in these circumstances and of the noxious condition of the snail-tainted ginger beer consumed by her, Mrs Donoghue appealed to the House of Lords. The five Lords who heard the case were divided as to the result, three being in favour of allowing the appeal, two being against it. Being a Scottish Appeal, two of the judges who heard the appeal were judges who had been trained in the law of Scotland, Lord MacMillan and Lord Thankerton. They were both in favour of allowing the appeal but the first judgement in favour of Mrs Donoghue was given by Lord Atkin and from him I quote:

> The liability for negligence, whether you style it such or treat it as in other systems as a species of 'culpa' is no doubt based on a general public sentiment on moral wrong-doing for which the offender must pay. But acts or omission which any moral code would censure cannot, in a practical world, be treated so as to give a right to every person injured by them to demand relief. In this way rules of law arise which limit the range of complainants and the extent of their remedy. The rule that you are to love your neighbour becomes in law, you must not injure your neighbour; and the lawyer's question, who is my neighbour? The answer seems to be – persons who are so closely and directly affected by my act that I ought reasonably to have them in contemplation as being so affected when I am directing my mind to the acts or omissions which are called in question.

In my professional life I have read and re-read these observations on, I suppose, many hundreds of occasions. I re-read them here to show Lord Atkin's sense that the civil law of negligence carried, to his mind, a relationship with moral wrongdoing and, of course, to show that his reasoning was illumined, if not directed, by the question that prompted the parable of the Good Samaritan and the parable itself.

I conclude, therefore, that there is some relationship between our secular law both in its civil and criminal aspects and biblical morality. And to further illustrate the sensitivity of Scottish judges to this matter in the past I quote the opinion of Lord Ardwall in *Middleton* v. *Tough*, 1908 (SC(J)) which was dealing with a case in which the occupier of a fishery was charged with failing to regard the due observance of the weekly close time which was imposed from 6 o'clock on Saturday afternoon to 6 o'clock on Monday morning when it was required that the netting of the leader of each and every bagnet should be entirely removed and taken out of the water. In this case the occupier of the fishery did not take the leaders of the bagnets out of the water during the whole of the specified closed period but left them there from 6 o'clock on Saturday evening until a very early time on Monday morning. The explanation was that at 6 o'clock on Saturday evening the state of the weather was such that it was physically impossible to remove the leaders, but by the Sunday the leaders could have been removed without danger and as a matter of fact one of them was removed by an employee of the Fishery Board but the occupier maintained that it would not be right to ask people to remove the leaders on the Sunday. It was to this aspect that Lord Ardwall's observation went:

> I should be very sorry if anything that we are deciding should seem in any way to derogate from the proper observance of Sunday. And I recommend the following view of the matter to these worthy people in Ross-shire who, greatly as I think to their credit, are desirous of avoiding unnecessary labour on the first day of the week. In the first place, I would point out that by leaving the net set for fishing all Sunday, the people who failed to remove the leaders are truly guilty of engaging in the industry of fishing the whole of the Sabbath day. In the next place, it may well be considered a work of necessity or mercy to lift the leaders of the nets on the Sabbath day. The phrase 'work of necessity or mercy', though embodied in a statute, is taken from the Confession of Faith and the Shorter Catechism, and these excellent documents profess to be founded on, and binding only so far as founded on, Scripture. Now, in Scripture I find direct authority to the effect that if a sheep fall into a pit on the Sabbath day, it is lawful to lay hold on it and lift it out. I hold that it is an analogous act to take up the leaders of salmon nets on the Sabbath day, and let out the unfortunate salmon which have been entrapped by an illegal net, and mercifully to restore them to their native freedom.

These are some illustrations of the relationship between the law and Christian ethics yesterday.

But I think it is manifest that the question for today is to what extent those who are responsible for making our laws are influenced by the principles of Christian ethics.

It is obvious as I have indicated earlier that Christian ethics go very much deeper than external acts or omissions but the biblical teaching on these is important as indicating limits to which the legislator can go. For example, I think it ought to be absolutely clear that no one should be compelled by law to do anything which is contrary to the principles of Christian ethics or the express commands of Scripture but it has to be remembered that no law enacted by man or even the moral law as given by God can of itself ensure compliance since sadly many breach God's moral law knowingly notwithstanding His Divine Commandment.

It has to be remembered that in a democracy the ultimate control of the laws, at least in their broad character, depends on the electorate. To the extent to which the government as representing the electorate has agreed to be bound by other legislative authorities, for example, the legislative authorities of the European Union and the Court of Justice of the European Union in Luxembourg or the judgements of the European Court of Human Rights at Strasbourg, the responsibility is, to a certain extent, less direct. On the other hand on the theory, which in my view is the correct theory, the ultimate responsibility for adhering to the judgements of Luxembourg and Strasbourg is a result of the action of government and parliament and their continuing acceptance of what emanates from Luxembourg and Strasbourg and therefore a continuing responsibility on the electorate here remains.

In our present circumstances as a nation we must take account of the fact that there are many people in our country who do not accept the authority of our Lord Jesus Christ and that by his own declaration his authority is of a spiritual kind and therefore it is not appropriate to attempt by secular law to force people to become Christians. On the other hand, it is the responsibility of Christians in our nation to do what they can to prevent dishonour to our Lord in our nation. For many years in the past it may have been generally accepted by our legislators that the fundamental law is the law of God with duties to God and our fellow human being the background to our law. If this was the position yesterday I do not think it is today. Now we have passed to a situation in which the background and, indeed with the passing of the Human Rights Act and the relevant provisions of the Scotland Act, the foreground has become a general structure of human rights which are expressed in very general terms which require interpretation by courts constituted by people with very different philosophical backgrounds. I illustrate simply one of the problems. The European Convention on Human Rights contains a provision for freedom of religion but I doubt whether the consequences of that for other aspects of life are capable of being reconciled. An individual's religion may have teaching on the nature of criminal punishments for particular offences and these may be capable of being characterised as inhuman or degrading. Capital punishment is perhaps the extreme example. Yesterday, in so far as the law of God was seen as fundamental with the duties imposed on human beings to respect and indeed love one another being the basis of the relationships between them, a satisfying unifying principle was provided. By focusing today on human rights as so described I venture to think that unifying principle has been lost, and internal tensions between the different human rights are created with no very clear principle provided for resolving such principles.

On the other hand, the present situation may give an argument to adherents of religions in respect of legislation by Parliament that was not available prior to our country being a party to the Human Rights Convention. Let me illustrate by reference to a contemporary question. At present a local authority is prevented by statute from promoting homosexuality and in its maintained schools from promoting it as an acceptable pattern of family life. Is it in accordance with the protection of religious freedom in the Convention now binding the Scottish Executive and Parliament to authorise a local authority to use its powers of local taxation to force a person who believes that the practice of homosexuality is sinful to pay money which is used for the purpose of promoting it? In Campbell and Cozans the court at Strasbourg held that it was a breach of the Convention for a school to use corporal punishment on a child whose parent objected to it as contrary to his or her religious or philosophical convictions. Would this also apply to promotion of homosexuality in teaching a child whose parents objected to it on religious or philosophical grounds?

I conclude by suggesting that there is a difference between the function of the Christian church in our nation at present and that of the legislator. The

11

legislator is faced with old problems but he is also faced with many new ones with the development of technology. Examples arise in relation to in vitro fertilisation and the development of techniques for gene modification (some of which have been the subject of control under the Human Fertilisation and Embryology Act) and the massive possibilities of modern communications and the internet, with its potential for transmitting pornography. The Christian church is God's witnessing people who acknowledge loyalty to Jesus Christ as their Head and are actuated by Christian love to God and to their fellow humans. I believe that danger arises if one mixes these two functions. Now our Confession makes clear that it is perfectly proper for a Christian to become a magistrate when called to that position and a magistrate in our Confession, I think, includes not only judicial functions but also legislative functions as well. I believe it is the function of the legislator, and particularly the Christian legislator, to do what can be done to provide justice and order in the state. He must recognise where this is the fact that there are people of different religious persuasions who are subject to the laws that are being proposed and account has to be taken in framing these laws of that fact. A good example occurs in relation to school assembly. I believe that it is perfectly proper for the legislature to require a Christian act of worship in every school at regular intervals to which the whole school is invited but allowing those of different religious persuasions freedom to exempt their children from that act of worship and if the numbers of such agreeing on an alternative form of worship is sufficient to make provision enabling them to have an act of worship in conformity with their views. The function of the Christian church on the other hand would be to provide, if called upon, assistance in the act of Christian worship and a witness both by word and action to the value of Christian principles so as, if possible, to persuade those who are not Christians to become so. In the words of Paul when before Agrippa when the latter said: 'Almost thou persuadest me to become a Christian,' Paul replied: 'I would to God, that not only thou, but also all that hear me this day, were both almost, and altogether such as I am except these bonds.'

In reality, in a democracy, the general pattern of the law will approximate to biblical standards to the extent to which the people are persuaded that these standards are right. But so long as there are people not so persuaded legislation may provide for them to the extent to which the preservation of peace and order is maintained. Obviously the more cohesive the society is in Christian belief the easier is the task of the Christian legislator. In my view the function of the Christian church is primarily to set out its beliefs and the value of them in word and action and in particular to manifest to those not professing the Christian faith that love to one's neighbour in word and action which Christian ethics enjoins. If the Church attempts to do the legislator's job for him or her there is a risk that by suggesting to the legislator what will be an appropriate way forward for legislation, the Church may obscure or appear to compromise the position in which itself believes.

If the Church states its position with regard to what it believes to be right it is for the legislator in my view to take account of that in framing proposed legislation for which proposals he will be responsible.

2

The Law and Theology in the Scots Tradition

Rev. Dr Finlay A. J. Macdonald
PRINCIPAL CLERK TO THE GENERAL ASSEMBLY OF THE CHURCH OF SCOTLAND

Lady Marion Fraser (chair) and Rev. Dr Finlay A. J. Macdonald

This is the second in a series of lectures under the general heading 'The Law and Christian Ethics'. The background to the series is the tension which exists 'between those perceptions that stem from a conscience informed by standards and values drawn from Scripture and Christian tradition and the standpoint of secular legislation which is largely determined by the spirit of the age; and between what the Christian sees as desirable and what in terms of legislation and politics is possible'. The concern which has prompted this lecture series is 'a recognition that our laws and institutions appear to be less related to Judeo-Christian traditions than in the past'.

My brief is to address these issues under the heading 'The Law and Theology in the Scots Tradition'. The title itself could give rise to not one, but a whole series of lectures, so it will be necessary to concentrate on one or two areas by way of example and illustration. Is there a single Scots tradition in either law or theology? Certainly there are points in our history where these two have interacted, sometimes happily, at other times less happily; and we shall come to these in due course.

Meantime, let us make a start by noting that while the title of the lecture

14

suggests that law and theology are two different disciplines (which indeed they are), there is also a very real sense in which law has been, and continues to be, regarded as an expression of theological truth. The first lesson in the theology I was taught in St Mary's College some thirty years ago differentiated between general and special revelation. In the world around us we have a general revelation of God as Creator but in Jesus Christ we have a distinctive, unique and special revelation of God as Saviour. And yet between creation and Christ there is that other quite distinctive revelation of the nature of God in the 'Torah', the law given to Moses at Mount Sinai. Now while, at one level, this law consists of the Ten Commandments and all the other moral and cultic regulations recorded in the Pentateuch, at another level it represents, in the words of David Granfield (article in *The New Dictionary of Theology*), 'an instrument of God's self communication'. The giving of the law is a twofold statement, namely that God wishes to be in relationship with His people and that He wishes His people to live in wholesome and creative relationships with each other. Thus the famous two tables of the law – those which regulate our duty to God and those which guide our duty to our neighbour. Aquinas speaks of law as being for the common good made by the one who has care of the community.

One of the great Reformation themes was, following Paul, to contrast law and gospel, works and faith. Paul's concern, particularly in Romans and Galatians, was that people misused the law to justify themselves and then to become filled with pride or despair at their works, whereas the proper focus was not on self, but on Christ. Salvation was to be found not in our own works of obedience to the law but in the life, death and resurrection of Jesus Christ. Luther went on to distinguish two uses of the law. The first, or civil use, is to offer a way, obedience to which will lead to a well ordered and peaceful community. The second, or theological use, drives us into an awareness of our sin, leading to despair as we contemplate our failures in obedience. This shows the limits of law, for in circumstances the answer is not yet more law. What we need then, in the words of David Keifert (*A New Handbook of Christian Theology*), is 'unconditional words of forgiveness, love, acceptance and hope from the only one who can speak without conditions; what we need is the gospel of Christ'. In the final analysis then we are condemned by law. Salvation is by God's grace alone.

But, of course, as well as Paul we have James, whose letter declaring that faith without works is dead, was described by Luther as 'a right strawy epistle'. We also have to recognise that Paul, for all his emphasis upon salvation by faith, still spoke of 'the law of Christ' and spoke warmly of those who fulfil that law. Jesus himself declared that he had come, not to abolish the law but to fulfil it and one of the Gospels (Matthew) clearly presents Jesus as a new Moses. Matthew's Jesus, like Moses, has to be hidden at birth from a murderous king, like Moses he comes out of Egypt, like Moses he delivers his law, his teaching from the mountain. Indeed, with its five blocks of teaching the first Gospel has a distinctively pentateuchal shape and, alone of all the Gospels, it deals with issues of discipline and law and order (dare one say practice and procedure!) within the life of the Church. Law is thus a significant element in the theology of both the Old and New Testaments.

Jesus, of course, for all that he proclaimed he had come, not to abolish but to fulfil the law, found himself at odds with those who understood it to be their duty to uphold the law. In essence the issue here was that alongside the Torah, the law as given to Moses, had grown up the Midrash. Hyam Maccoby (*Judaism in the First Century*, p. 4) explains that whereas the Sadduccees thought that God's Word as given required no supplement, the Pharisees considered that revelation was a two-way process, comprising God's Word and human response. 'Midrash' means 'searching' and through the midrashic, pharisaic tradition there evolved an authoritative interpretation of the Torah. It was with this tradition that Jesus came into conflict on occasions such as the controversy over eating food with unwashed hands and healing on the Sabbath. It would appear that for Jesus there were different levels of law. Ritual, cultic and ceremonial regulation was not to be accorded the same status as the great life-affirming principles of the Torah as revelation of God, a revelation now fulfilled in him. To heal on the Sabbath was not to set aside the law but to affirm the greater truth that the Sabbath was made for man and not man for the Sabbath.

This appreciation of different levels of law is an important one, though one with which we need to be careful. Some months ago there was a case which received considerable publicity. It concerned a woman who lodged a defence of necessity in a drink-driving case. She maintained that she drove her car, albeit she was over the drink-driving limit, as the only means available to her to escape from a man who had raped her. In accepting the defence the sheriff allowed that there can be occasions when the demands of justice mean that man-made laws have to yield to higher principles. This example allows us to note that there is an important, indeed a vital element in both theology and law, namely, justice. The law has to do with the administration of justice, and in theology also we have, in recent years particularly, seen a strong emphasis on concepts such as social justice and liberation theology. The anti-apartheid movement in South Africa and the civil rights movement in the United States both had powerfully strong theological underpinning. Alongside the Hebrew concept of 'Torah', therefore, we have the concepts of 'mishpat' meaning 'judgement' (which being the judgement of God is understood as being inherently just) and 'tsedeq' meaning 'righteous', that is to say, doing that which is right in God's eyes. God required not simply obedience to regulations but a commitment to a just society and a just society was, by definition, a society ordered in accordance with the divine will and purpose. 'Let justice roll down like waters and righteousness like an ever-flowing stream,' said Amos, and with equal eloquence Micah asked 'What does the Lord require of you but to do justly, to love mercy and to walk humbly with your God?' In the theology of the New Testament the concept of 'dikaiosoune' (righteousness) is likewise important – not the righteousness that we would more properly call self-righteousness, but the righteousness which reflects living in a right and healthy relationship with God and neighbour. Blessed are those who hunger and thirst after such righteousness, for they shall be filled.

Earlier we noted the underlying Torah/law assumptions of Matthew's Gospel with Jesus presented as the new Moses. By way of comparison we might say that Luke's Gospel reflects mishpat/justice principles with Jesus cast very much in the prophetic tradition as the new Samuel. The radical Song of Mary (the Magnificat) echoes the song of Hannah; the presentation in the temple recalls the child Samuel with Simeon taking the place of the old priest Eli. Further, Luke's Gospel, written from the Gentile perspective, seeks to enlarge the frontiers of God's kingdom – there is place for sinners, for Samaritans, for prodigals, for Zacchaeus, for the one in a hundred who is 'out on the hills astray, far off from the gates of gold'. Here is liberation theology and judgement which does not condemn; here is justice tempered with mercy and the manifesto of a new kind of kingdom of God. Moses and Samuel appear on the mount of

Transfiguration but both defer to Jesus for in him both law and prophecy find their fulfilment.

Over the years I have heard many words spoken in many General Assemblies, some of which I remember. Among these are a response given by Tom Morton, when he was Convener of the Board of Social Responsibility, to a suggestion that only members of the Church of Scotland should be accommodated in Church Eventide Homes. Tom was appalled and reminded the Assembly that the Church was in the business of caring for 'the last and the least and the lost'. When I was in a parish in Glasgow, I shared for a couple of years with Noel Donnelly in teaching a Scripture and Life Course at the Craighead Institute. I remember how Noel used to describe Luke's Gospel as the gospel for the 'wee folk' (and he wasn't just thinking of Zacchaeus), reflecting the recurring prophetic call not for a mechanical, ritualistic, narrow obedience to God's law, but for the larger and broader application of principles of justice and fairness for all. In the words of Frederick William Faber:

> For the love of God is broader
> Than the measures of our mind;
> And the heart of the Eternal
> Is most wonderfully kind.
>
> But we make his love too narrow
> By false limits of our own,
> And we magnify his strictness
> With a zeal he will not own.

It is precisely here that we find theology and law sharing a common purpose. Luke's importunate widow may have had to keep nagging the judge, but the parable highlights the principle that all are equal, not only before God, but before the law, and neither God, nor the law, has any favourites.

But let us now try to bring in the Scots tradition, or at least the Scottish dimension. We have in this country an ecclesiastical history going back some 1600 years – the Church of Ninian, and of Columba, the medieval church, the Reformation tradition, the present-day plurality of Christian traditions and the ecumenical theology which has been such a characteristic of this century and to which Scotland has been a major contributor. We cannot possibly enter into a consideration of the whole sweep of Scottish theological thought, even were I competent to engage in such an exercise, which I am not. I will focus on some aspects of that tradition with which I am most familiar, namely the reformed, the Protestant and the Presbyterian, but let us all be aware that there is much, much more.

It is generally accepted that the Scottish legal tradition as we understand it today begins with Stair, Sir James Dalrymple of Stair, afterwards created Viscount Stair by William III. Stair was Lord President of the Court of Session and in 1681 published the first edition of *The Institutions of the Law of Scotland*. Alastair Macintyre in his *Whose Justice? Which Rationality?* describes Stair's theoretical and conceptual scheme as one which 'expressed in terms of the law of Scotland not only the legal, but also the key theological and philosophical doctrines concerning justice, law and rational and right conduct'. In other words, Stair's scheme is essentially theological. My distinguished predecessor as Principal Clerk, James Weatherhead, in the introductory chapter to his *The Constitution and Laws of the Church of Scotland* takes up this point and notes that Stair speaks of the divine law, or law of nature 'written by the finger of God upon man's heart'.

Stair's model was Justinian's *Institutions*, though he was also familiar with contemporary European jurisprudence. Justinian, the sixth-century Roman emperor, had enumerated three common precepts which are set forth in the civil law: to live honestly, to wrong no man and to give every man his right, principles enunciated in the thirteenth chapter of the letter to Romans. Justinian further taught that reason apprehends first principles of law of two kinds, those of equity or right and those of the good, useful or expedient. Following this distinction Stair maintains that this first type of law, the law of equity or right, itself reflects three first principles, namely (1) that God is to be obeyed by man, (2) that man is a free creature, having power to dispose of himself and all things, insofar as by his obedience to God he is not restrained and (3) that this freedom of man is in his own power. In the exercise of this power human beings make laws for the better ordering of human societies. Essentially, there are two types of law – the God-given and the man-made; or, putting it another way, natural law and positive law; or putting it yet another way, the law of equity and fundamental precepts and the law of expediency. This second type of law, the human-made law, is necessary only because of the fall. Because, Stair argues, human beings are in rebellion against God and the principles of equity it is profitable for them 'to find out expedients and helps to make equity effectual; and therefore to make upon societies of men, that they may mutually defend one another and procure to one another their rights'. One can see in all of this the seeds of political philosophy of Locke and Hobbes with their theories of social contract, something which resonates with such familiar Scottish ideas as claims of right, constitutional monarchy and sovereignty of the people.

Macintyre makes two interesting comparisons with Stair's theory. The first is with Justinian. Macintyre notes that Stair explicitly departs from Justinian's view of the priority of legal obligations. Justinian and Roman law generally had categorised the concerns of law in terms of persons, things and actions. Against this Stair held that the proper object of law is the right itself, whether it concerns persons, things or actions.

The second comparison Macintyre offers is with the work of the English jurist, Sir William Blackstone, who published his commentaries on the Laws of England in 1765 – more than half a century after Stair. Unlike Stair, Blackstone did not deduce the first principles of law from theological or metaphysical doctrine but maintained rather that God had 'graciously reduced the rule of obedience to this one paternal precept, "that man should pursue his own true and substantial happiness".' Blackstone, further, laid great emphasis on precedent: 'The doctrine of the law is this; that precedent and rules must be followed, unless flatly absurd or unjust; for though their reason be not obvious at first view, yet we owe such a deference to former times as not to suppose that they acted wholly without consideration.'

Macintyre notes three areas of sharp contrast between Stair and Blackstone, the Scots and the English traditions. First, with regard to appeals to equity, Blackstone would allow these only when a case arises which the established rules did not cover and where precedent was silent. For Stair, by contrast, the rules of equity were among the first principles of justice and indeed these could be appealed to *against* established rule and precedent.

A second area of difference concerned property. Blackstone absolutised the rights of property so that social obligations depended largely upon the individual's place within established property relationships. By contrast, Stair made the treatment and the status of obligations prior to the treatment and status of property so that obligations can be imposed upon and constrain the property owner.

The third area of difference has to do with the relationship between theology and law. God is not excluded from Blackstone's scheme, though he does in effect exclude himself by 'reducing the rule of obedience to this one paternal precept: "that man should pursue his own true and substantial happiness".' By contrast, as Macintyre puts it: 'in Stair's *Institutions* the theology cannot be excised without irreparable damage to the whole'. This last point resonates with the observations of Lord Mackay in the previous lecture in this series to the effect that the Sixth, Eighth and Ninth Commandments were not elaborated in Scots law but taken as read, whereas in the English tradition much more detailed expositions were developed.

We need now to look at the practical interaction of law and theology in the Scots tradition, having regard to the caveat already entered, namely that this will, of necessity, be highly selective. My particular area of interest, and therefore the focus of what I have to say, concerns the post-Reformation Church of Scotland, but we need also to acknowledge that there is a larger Scots tradition than that.

There are a number of areas where we can see an interaction of theology and law. There is, for example, the whole thrust of much post-Reformation theology, with its emphasis on the idea of the covenant between God and man. This, of course, arises from the Old Testament idea of a covenant relationship between God and his people and in turn gave rise to theological thinking and ecclesiastical arrangements expressed in terms of legal models. There is an Old Testament understanding of the relationship between the people and God. So, we find such significant points in our ecclesiastical history as the National Covenant, the Solemn League and Covenant and, arising from this, the sense of Scotland as a covenanted people, rather like ancient Israel. The underlying assumptions for some two centuries after the Reformation was that to be a Scot was to be a member of the Kirk as the expression of the spiritual kingdom within the realm. And, indeed, this was no more than a carry-over of pre-Reformation assumptions concerning the relationship between the pre-Reformation Church and the people. The notion of a diverse, disparate, multi-cultural society is relatively recent. Even the Declaratory Articles appended to the Church of Scotland Act 1921 talk fairly naturally of the 'Christian faith of the

Scottish people'. That is not a phrase which trips so comfortably off the tongue today.

Another area where we see an interaction of law and theology is in the eighteenth century phenomenon known, pejoratively, as 'legal preaching'. The 'legal preachers' tended to focus on issues such as duty and moral obligations within the community, compared with the evangelical preachers who stressed the importance of our relationship with God, emphasising now the sweetness of communion with Christ, now the terrors which awaited the damned. These were the preachers who attracted the crowds at the Holy Fairs. Apart from not being 'crowd-pullers' the more considered criticism of the 'legal preachers' was that by concentrating on our duties one to another, by focusing on what we would today call Christian Ethics, they were encouraging people to rely on good works and not laying enough emphasis on man's fallen nature and utter reliance upon the grace of Christ.

The legal model even found its way into the theological writing of the period. For example, Professor Blackwell, Professor of Theology at Aberdeen in the early eighteenth century, recounted in his 'Scheme Sacrum' of 1712, how the Deity did from all eternity enjoy perfect blessedness in the 'contemplation of his own perfection'. But then the Divine Mind found that he could get 'an additional revenue of glory by creating rational creatures who should sing eternal hallelujahs'. Blackwell continues: 'A motion was made to this effect in the Council of Three-in-One and the aforesaid motion was agreed to.' Henry Grey Graham in his *Social Life of Scotland in the Eighteenth Century* remarks: 'so states Dr Blackwell who attributes to the deliberations of the Trinity the procedure of the Presbytery of Aberdeen' (p. 396).

Another area where we see the interaction of law and theology, and an area particularly relevant to this lecture series, is the area of church and state. The issue of church/state relations has been a recurring theme in the ecclesiastical and political life of Scotland. In 574AD Columba ordained Aidan as king of Dalriada with the wonderful prayer: 'Believe firmly, O Aidan, that none of your adversaries will be able to resist you unless you first deal falsely against me or my relatives in Ireland' (Burleigh, *A Church History of Scotland*, p. 18). Characters from the medieval church as diverse as Queen Margaret and Cardinal David Beaton both exercised great power in church and state and the Reformation of August 1560 was an act not of the Scottish Church but of the Scottish Parliament. In our own time, questions such as religious representation in a reformed House of Lords and the nature of prayer in the Scottish Parliament reflect the ongoing relationship between church and state.

However, there is a particular aspect of church/state relations which brings into very sharp focus the interaction of law and theology and that has to do with the church's creed or doctrine. A meeting of the Scots Parliament on 1 August 1560 received a supplication listing various grievances against the church. In response to this the parliament invited the petitioners 'to draw in plain and several heads the sum of that doctrine which they would maintain, and would desire that the present parliament would establish as wholesome, true and necessary to be believed and to be received within that realm'. Within four days the petitioners, John Knox and colleagues had drawn up the Scots Confession and, on 17 August, it was ratified by the Parliament 'as wholesome and sound doctrine, grounded upon the infallible truth of God's word'. Seven years later, with the exile of Queen Mary and the establishment of a Protestant regency on behalf of the infant King James, Parliament, having given legislative sanction to Protestant doctrine, now went on to recognise the Protestant church as 'the only true and holy kirk of Jesus Christ within this realm'. Eighty years later, in 1647, the General Assembly adopted the Westminster Confession of Faith and that in turn become incorporated into parliamentary statutes such as an act of 1690 'Ratifying the Confession of Faith and Settling the Presbyterian Church Government' and splendidly titled 1693 'Act for Settling the Quiet and Peace of the Church'. The Church's faith had found its way into the law of the land; a theological statement had become a constitutional document, something from which much ecclesiastical conflict and civil litigation was to flow. The influence of the Kirk was further demonstrated by the enactment of the 1706 Act of Security as a means of securing not only the position of the Kirk, but also securing its acquiescence, if not support, in the proposed union of the parliaments of Scotland and England. This act, a parallel measure to the Act of Settlement south of the border, is annually confirmed in the Queen's letter to the General Assembly.

This power of the Kirk in the period of the union of the parliaments and the binding together of law and theology can be seen in two quite different cases which are worth recounting briefly.

One is the sad and shameful case of Thomas Aitkenhead. In 1695 the Scots

Parliament had ratified an older statute making blasphemy a capital offence. And Aitkenhead fell foul of this provision. He was eighteen years old and on Christmas Eve 1696 he was sentenced to death for describing theology as 'a rhapsody of feigned and ill-invented nonsense' and referring to the Old Testament as 'Ezra's fables' and to the New Testament as 'The History of the Impostor Christ'. Despite his plea for clemency on the grounds of his tender years and on the basis that he had merely reiterated what he had read in books, and despite further a readiness to declare his faith and to resolve 'by the assistance of Almighty God, to make my abhorrence of what is contained in this libel appear to the world in my subsequent life and conversation', the sentence of death was carried out. An extreme and not typical case, but a terrifying example of the power of the sword being invoked in defence of the faith – of the sanctions of civil law being applied in support of theology.

The other case, a decade after Aitkenhead, concerned James Greenshields. Greenshields was an Episcopalian who opened a meeting house in Edinburgh opposite St Giles and there conducted services according to the Book of Common Prayer. His landlord objected and Greenshield was evicted. However, he found new premises and the services continued. At this point the Presbytery of Edinburgh intervened and ordered him to desist, but he declined their jurisdiction. The Presbytery appealed to the civil power and Greenshields was arrested and sent to the Tolbooth. The Court of Session held that 'there needs no law condemning the English service, for introducing the Presbyterian worship explodes it as inconsistent'. We can also recall the 1567 Act which recognised 'only one true and holy kirk within the realm'. However, Greenshields, taking advantage of the recent Act of Union, appealed to the House of Lords and was successful. In 1711 the Lords reversed the judgement of the Court of Session and ordered the Edinburgh magistrates (not the presbytery) to pay the costs. The same year saw the enactment of the Toleration Act which gave official recognition to the separate and distinctive Scottish Episcopal Church. There was no longer 'only one true and holy kirk within the realm'. Twenty-two years later the first Secession further undermined the Kirk's monopoly.

Now there are many stories in this vein with which we could while away the evening. The point is that they illustrate a negative aspect of which we need to be aware in the history of the relationship between theology and law. They also challenge us to acknowledge a distinction between the Church as political institution within society and the Church as bearer of the authentic Christian tradition within society. This in turn leads us to face up to the hard question – 'Have we sometimes abused the influence we have had and thereby ourselves contributed to the marginalisation of the Judaeo-Christian tradition in public policy formation and decision making?' Or is there a different question in there, in some ways a harder question for us, namely: 'Are we all agreed in our understanding of our tradition and what that tradition has to offer to the legislative process?' It is very clear that on a number of social issues Christians hold differing views. The debate on Clause 28 or 2A has highlighted divisions not only within society but disagreements within the churches. Indeed, experience and observation of a number of churches around the world indicates that there is no more painful or divisive issue for the churches than the issue of homosexuality.

We are also very aware of the ongoing debate over the interpretation of Scripture and the relationship of the Scriptures to the Word of God – whether as container of that Word or as identified with that Word, without remainder. Certainly 2000 years of Christian history shows that the defenders of the faith have not always been right and I certainly know of no doctrine of the infallibility of General Assembly majorities. A century and more ago our forebears prosecuted men like John Macleod Campbell, Edward Irving and William Robertson Smith whose heresies are now our orthodoxies. And yet, to use a well-worn phrase, there are 'core values'. For example, the commandment which forbids adultery reflects a culture where the issue was primarily one of property, yet the timeless wisdom of the commandment is as valid in our very different culture which affirms equality of personhood between men and women. And while the cases of Greenshields and Aitkenhead represent the negative aspects of theological/legal co-operation our history also records more positive aspects. Indeed Tom Devine in his recent *The Scottish Nation* shows in a chapter on Religion and Society that, contrary to popular belief, religious values continued to influence Scottish politics during the process of urbanisation and industrialisation. For example, Devine goes so far as to describe Thomas Chalmers as 'possibly the most influential Scot of the nineteenth century' (p. 364), and notes the significance of the Christian commitment of men like Keir Hardie and John Wheatley.

I have endeavoured in this lecture to reflect on a number of areas in which it seems to me that law and theology have interacted within our Scottish tradition, for good or ill. I would like now to conclude with one further and highly contemporary example which raises issues for both law and theology. I refer to the question of human rights, the subject of a specific lecture later in the series. Indeed, it would appear that it is the law itself which has been most affected by the incorporation of the European Convention on Human Rights into Scots Law through the Scotland Act. Moreover, it is a measure of the interest in the matter that a seminar on the Churches and Human Rights held in Strasbourg and hosted by the Moderator brought together a significant representation of clergy and lawyers and enabled those of us who participated to engage directly with representatives of the Court there. Stewart Lamont, reporting on the event in *The Herald*, chose an equestrian image but then couldn't decide whether it was a case of hearing it from the horse's mouth or cleansing the stables. At least he didn't suggest a belated locking of the stable door!

One of the outcomes of the tensions between church and state, between theology and law, has been a recognition of the independent jurisdiction in matters spiritual of the Church of Scotland. The civil courts will not interfere in matters of worship, government, doctrine and discipline. An act of Parliament, the Church of Scotland Act, 1921, gives legislative force to this, though it is also important to note that the act specifically affirms that nothing in it 'shall prejudice the recognition of any other Church in Scotland as a Christian Church protected by law in the exercise of its spiritual functions'. (There's a lot of history between 1567 and 1921!)

When, two years ago, the government introduced the bill to incorporate the European Convention of Human Rights into UK law, the Church sought clarification as to how this might impinge upon its independent spiritual jurisdiction. Could the civil courts interfere in spiritual matters if it were alleged that human rights issues were involved? For reasons we don't need to go into here it was felt that this was unlikely and, indeed, the government, through a statement in parliament, made clear that it was not its intention to disturb the present constitutional settlement between church and state (though presumably it was not the government's intention to get rid of temporary sheriffs either!). However, what is interesting is that the General Assembly of 1998 was not only extremely vigorous in defending its jurisdictional freedom, it was also most

26

anxious to ensure that the Church's procedures reflected, as far as possible, the principles of the European Convention. As a consequence there is currently underway a review of disciplinary procedures. Arguably, if the Church does indeed have an independent spiritual jurisdiction this may not be required in law. However, theological factors also come into play for human rights have a theological as well as a legal dimension. Both theology and law, as we noted earlier, have a common concern with justice. In a similar kind of way I found myself in 1999, along with Dr Alison Elliott, Convener of the Church and Nation Committee, giving evidence to the Royal Commission on Reform of the House of Lords. We were both intrigued that the Commissioners appeared to have some difficulty in appreciating that we were not there with a single-minded purpose of securing the best deal for the Church of Scotland, but to offer reflections from a Christian theological perspective on what might be the best arrangements for the good of the nation.

The title of this lecture is 'The Law and Theology in the Scots Tradition'. Over the centuries there have been shifts of theological emphasis – the creation theology of the Celtic Church, the medieval theologies of Thomas Aquinas and Duns Scotus, the insights of Luther and Calvin, the Scots Confession and the Westminster Confession, Arminianism, Socinanism, old light and new light. One generation's heresy is the next generation's orthodoxy. And yet that is far from saying that all is relative. One of my favourite statements arising out of a Church's struggle to express the truth it believes and proclaims is to be found in the revised testimony of the anti-burgher seceders who in 1804, in the midst of the new light controversy, struggled with their relationship to the Westminster Confession and related documents and came up with the following declaration:

> Though we acknowledge these as subordinate standards, they are not at all the rule of what we are bound to believe, but a public declaration of what we do believe. That is no human composure, however, excellent and well expressed, can be supposed to contain a full and comprehensive view of divine truth; so by this adherence, we are not precluded from embracing, upon due deliberation, any further light which may afterward arise from the word of God about any article of divine truth.

It is in this spirit that I would suggest that the Church and the faith continue to have a vital role in underpinning the values of a healthy society. Few would seriously argue today that such a society is one in which those who disagree with the Church's teaching should be punished by the civil power. This is not the sort of relationship we seek between theology and law, between church and state. Our aim is for something more positive, where the timeless insights of the Scriptures and values of the Gospel are harnessed by theologians, politicians and lawyers working towards

> The day in whose clear-shining light
> All wrong shall stand revealed,
> When justice shall be throned with might,
> And every hurt be healed;
>
> When knowledge, hand in hand with peace
> Shall walk the earth abroad
> The day of perfect righteousness
> The promised day of God.
>
> (Frederick Lucian Hosmer)

3
Human Rights Law

Alan Miller
PROFESSOR OF LAW, UNIVERSITY OF STRATHCLYDE

Prof. Alan Miller and Dr Alison Elliott (chair)

I am delighted to have been invited to make a contribution to this interesting series of public lectures on The Law and Christian Ethics organised by the Church of Scotland Board of Social Responsibility and the Centre for Theology and Public Issues. It is a delight because it enables me to take a step back from the cut and thrust of practising and teaching law to reflect upon the potential development of human rights and human rights law in the next century and how the Church may relate to such development. I note from the information explaining the series of lectures that there is reference to 'the standpoint of secular legislation which is largely determined by the spirit of the age'. It is this theme which I would like to explore by attempting to reflect what may be the cutting edge of the development of human rights and human rights law as reflecting the spirit of the age which may influence secular legislation.

It is inevitable that the relationship between the Church and the law in this new century is an issue demanding exploration if only because of the shared interplay between the Church and the law in recent centuries in which the issues of sovereignty and of rights have been central in shaping Scotland's constitutional development right up until the present day.

In particular, I was intrigued by the fact that this series was being held in part by the board of Social Responsibility. It does appear to me that this also quite naturally raises the question of what it is to be socially responsible in this new century and how, indeed, the twenty-first century shall judge the Church as to how it has exercised social responsibility. Generally speaking in law, and in particular under the European Convention on Human Rights, and in a sense also within the Church you are entitled to know how you are to be judged, to receive a reasoned judgement and for this judgement to come at the end. Well, I want to raise at the beginning that the Church will come to be judged by the twenty-first century as to whether it exercised in deeds and not only words social responsibility in response to the demands of the times, or to the 'spirit of the age'. The answer to this question may well determine the extent of the relevance of the Church and indeed of any other institution in this new century.

To determine then what it is to be socially responsible in the twenty-first century, it may be helpful to consider a historical and global context as well as the national context.

HISTORIC AND GLOBAL CONTEXT

In taking a step back then from the cut and thrust of daily life as a human rights lawyer and surveying the complex processes unfolding around the world what does appear to be emerging as a basic issue is that at the dawn of the twenty-first century society has reached an impasse similar to that in the eighteenth century.

It was in the eighteenth century that the old order of feudal relations of society was blocking progress and holding back the ascendant class of merchants and industrialists. It was these new emerging forces which were demanding the right to lay claim on the available and potential resources of society. In these circumstances what became essential to be developed was a new definition of sovereignty and rights with which these new forces could equip themselves to challenge the old order. Such a definition came to be provided by Rousseau and others from the Enlightenment and the concepts and slogans of 'liberty, equality and fraternity' are still in everyday language today. In these times the significance of such a definition of sovereignty and rights was that it represented the affirmation of the right of private property over the feudal relations of society. It was the affirmation of this right of private property which released the dynamic of enterprise, trade and commerce which have propelled the last two centuries through an unprecedented turmoil in development in economic, technological capacity etc.

Events unfolding do appear to indicate that we may now have reached another similar impasse with the existing order blocking further progress of society. I refer not simply to the recent events in Seattle with the World Trade Organisation but draw upon the experience of a number of major world conferences held by the United Nations over this past decade. These would include the World Conference on the environment in Rio which became known as the Earth Summit; the World Conference on Food in Rome; the World Conference on Women in Beijing; and the World Conference on Human Rights in Vienna. It is no exaggeration to say that at all of these conferences the common theme was that the demands of humanity were placed on the table but the existing order did not meet such demands. The Earth Summit could not remove the crippling debt burden on the developing countries, the Food Conference could not give food to the masses of humanity and the Women's Conference recognised their degraded status. The eighteenth-century Louis XIV's self-serving definition of rights as 'L'état, c'est moi!' reappeared at Rome when the US representative proclaimed contempt for international human rights treaties by declaring that 'there is no right to food'. Just today by coincidence in this new century we are marking International Water Day and it would appear that the theme of these world conferences of the last decade of the twentieth century is being continued. Today marks the end of the Second World Water Forum. Water experts believe that one billion people worldwide lack safe drinking water and that three billion do not have adequate sanitation. Reuters report today in our press, however, that the concluding Forum has avoided concrete measures to ensure clean water for the world's growing population but has agreed instead on a set of guidelines for governments. The Reuters correspondent quotes from a protester who summed up this outcome by declaring that 'if you say it is a human right, you change the whole framework. Then you can't trade it as a commodity and make profit.'

Increasing numbers of protesters and commentators are now stating that on a global basis there has been reached an impasse between property rights and human rights. They have claimed that the exercise of property rights won back in the eighteenth century is no longer a progressive force but is retrogressive as

31

it is causing the marginalisation and disempowerment of humanity itself. They have claimed that if the block to progress in the eighteenth century was feudal relations then the block on progress three centuries later is represented by such bodies as the International Monetary Fund, the World Bank, the World Trade Organisation, etc. Such critics argue that the eighteenth-century slogans of emancipation of liberty, equality and fraternity have been replaced by slogans of free market, pluralism and human rights but that these new slogans are rhetoric, and deployed to preserve the status quo. Such critics claim that rather than there being free markets there are, in fact, nations being controlled by multinational co-operations; that rather than there being pluralism and respect for autonomy and self-determination there is a system of certain powers decree-ing smaller states which are unco-operative to be 'rogue states' and labelling them as being sponsors of terrorism and of Islamic fundamentalism etc; that rather than human rights what there is in the real world is, in fact, the trampling underfoot of even such fundamental rights as the right to life itself, and that this is justified by the 'trickle-down' philosophy which espouses the view that wealth creation of multinational corporations will generate a trickle-down of benefits to the masses of humanity.

Those who claim that such an impasse similar to the eighteenth century has again been reached also would point to conditions which are giving rise to a challenge to the prevailing order in a fashion similar to that in the eighteenth century. It is pointed out that one of the triumphs of the twentieth century was the rise of democratic consciousness and the awareness of the need of modern definitions and guarantees of sovereignty and of rights if society was to pro-gress and the needs of the masses of humanity be addressed.

This certainly was the central issue at the World Conference on Human Rights in Vienna in 1993 when indeed such a modern definition of rights began to emerge. Although such a modern definition has yet to be fully expressed and realised some of its features may already be identifiable. One feature would certainly appear to be that rights are human rights because simply by virtue of humanity each of us enjoys rights which are inalienable such as the right to be, the right to develop a personality. Another feature would be that such inalien-able rights are civil, political, economic, social and cultural and that these are indivisible and inter-related and it is only the guarantee of such rights in an integral manner which can enable each of us to affirm our right to personality.

32

Another feature would be that such a definition of rights is placed at the centre of the development of society and not reduced to a mere aspiration or abstract ideal. In furtherance of this such a definition would lead to a mandate upon states which have ratified international human rights treaties to implement such treaties through legislation and policies, and not reduce the rights to long-term policy objectives etc.

What appears to be clearly emerging in the past recent period at the end of the twentieth century and the beginning of the twenty-first century is the demand that if society is to progress and the needs of today are to be met by the available and potential resources then it is such a modern definition which is required.

Of course, human rights very clearly bring together not only the law and the Church but the law and politics. Accordingly a basic issue which has emerged in these times is that the affirmation of such a human right to a society fit to live in requires the means of effectively participating in the decision-making process and this is why democratic renewal, within and among nations, has become the call of modern times.

NATIONAL CONTEXT

Scotland has, of course, been travelling down its own road towards democratic renewal. The Scotland Act 1998 and the Human Rights Act 1998 were the result of the demands of the twentieth century for self-determination 'as individual citizens and as a people'. This most fundamental change for the past three centuries in our constitutional legal system has enabled the beginning of the development of a modern human rights agenda as part of democratic renewal in Scotland and indeed throughout the United Kingdom. The Scottish Parliament has significant legislative powers, has the responsibility of implementing United Nations Treaties on human rights and, of course, the Parliament's sovereignty by the civil and political rights guaranteed by the European Convention on Human Rights. There are, of course, significant limitations concerning both the Scotland Act and the Human Rights Act but in the historical context these limitations are of a secondary nature and the real issue is the potential of the development of a modern democratic Scottish personality reflecting our own traditions but also being in tune with the universal needs and experiences of humanity.

The Scottish constitutional tradition on sovereignty is that of a limited sovereignty and not of an absolute sovereignty which has become the UK theory and practice. The modern expression of the Scottish constitutional tradition of limited sovereignty is that of popular sovereignty, that is sovereignty lying with the people. In parallel, the constitutional Scottish tradition of rights is also distinctive in that it has viewed rights as a right to a personality which the individual cannot fulfil other than in a community which recognises such a right. This also contrasts with the Anglo-American notion of civil liberties and the relationship between the individual and the state, as opposed to viewing the individual as a person standing in a community and able to be emancipated only to the extent of the degree of emancipation of the community itself.

It does appear that there is a potential that if Scotland continues down the road of democratic renewal and a modern democratic Scottish personality does develop then it will be one which very much strikes a chord with the universal experience and need of this time, which is that of sovereignty resting with the people and the human rights of each human being affirmed. Of course, there is a long way to proceed down this road towards democratic renewal and there are few certainties concerning the travel but one thing which is certain is that if there is real progress on this road of democratic renewal then the results will be illuminated well beyond our borders. This is because the questions of democratic renewal and of human rights are 'the spirit of our age' and whosoever makes progress will be effectively contributing towards the progress of humanity as a whole and the advance of society in general. Although a small nation, Scotland may be well placed to make some contribution – developing upon its rich legacy in the eighteenty-century Age of Enlightenment out of all proportion to its size, with the European identity as one of the most ancient nations and with no problem of ethnicity of violence, standing within the Westminster Parliamentary system and its Commonwealth identity and, of course, now assuming the responsibilities to implement the United Nations International Human Rights Treaties.

THE CHURCH

The Church, of course, has been no stranger to these issues of sovereignty, rights and enlightenment. It has had a huge influence upon the development of these matters within Scottish history right up to and including the modern Claim of Right of 1989. The Church has also secured for itself a right of conscience.

What, then, does it mean for the Church to be socially responsible in the twenty-first century? Well, in general terms, it may mean that the responsibility of the Church is to extend recognition of right of conscience to society as a whole as a basis of modern citizenship and society. An individual right to conscience cannot flourish without the society itself being so constituted.

To be socially responsible, therefore, may mean to identify with the needs of a modern human-rights agenda as the affirmation of humanity, the human-isation of our social and natural environment. The 'spirit of our age' requires such a modern human-rights agenda to be affirmed in the here and now, in deeds as well as words and not simply as a Christian ethic or as merely a long-term aspiration but as a constitutional and political guarantee in a modern society.

It may be that it is in this field that the Church will have to hoist its standard and claim its relevance as an institution in an increasingly secular and chal-lenging society. It may be submitted that to do so is to be no more than true to the Church's own tradition and identity and indeed to give such a modern expression in these changing times. It is in this sense that the Church, as with any other institution, may come to be judged by the twenty-first century.

4

The Law and Christian Ethics in Business

Stephen Copp[1]
EUROPEAN CENTRE FOR CORPORATE GOVERNANCE
BOURNEMOUTH UNIVERSITY

Stephen Copp (chair: Margaret McIntosh)

This chapter is based on a lecture which formed part of a series on the Law and Christian Ethics. The series originated out of a concern that the law is moving away from the Judaeo-Christian values which influenced its development. This chapter focuses on business. Business is a perennial source of topical issues with an ethical twist yet headline issues can present a distorted picture. In developing a Christian perspective on law and business it is important that a rigorous and robust framework is developed, based on clear ideas as to its purpose, its principles and its problems. This chapter will set out how such a framework might be constructed and how it might be applied to a contemporary legal and business problem of some importance: the role and regulation of the company director. The role of the director is central to the governance of businesses of all sizes and of crucial economic importance. The limits of acceptable conduct by directors have been established over an extended period of time by Parliament and the Courts, not just in company law but in fields as seemingly diverse as competition law, employment law and environmental law. However, there has been much heated debate as to two central questions: whether directors should be responsible to their company's shareholders or to a wider range of interested parties; and what responsibilities a director should actually have. These issues have now been extensively considered by the Law Commission and the Company Law Review Steering Group. The processes have proven controversial, not least because they have provided an opportunity to examine the assumptions and values on which the law might be based. This chapter will show that while many of the assumptions and values relied upon are not inconsistent with a Christian framework they are ideologically flawed. Not least, from a Christian perspective, they provide no adequate answer to the problem of mankind's sinfulness.

CARS, CLOSURES AND DOT.COMS

April 2000 was an interesting month to deliver a lecture on 'The Law and Christian Ethics in Business'! During this month four stories with a business element ran and ran in the media. The proposed disposal by BMW of its interest in Rover cars to Alchemy, or, perhaps, to Phoenix.[2] The closure by Barclays Bank plc of some 172 branches.[3] The recent dramatic fall in the share price of some of the dot.com companies. In the same week Standard Life, based in Edinburgh, where the lecture was being delivered, agreed to hold a special meeting to consider five resolutions put forward by Fred Woollard which would result in its demutualisation and possible flotation on the Stock Exchange.[4] Each of these provoked strong responses and heated debates. All were seen in different ways as giving rise to questions over the law and ethics of business. What would happen to Rover's employees, and, of course, their families? The Alchemy bid might lead to 7,500 direct job losses and 19,000 to 45,000 indirect job losses; the Phoenix bid to 2,000 and 8,000 respectively. What would happen to the communities which would no longer have ready access to a bank in their midst? There were claims that eighty villages would be left without a bank branch. How could these closures be reconciled with the revelation that Barclays' chairman, Sir Peter Middleton, had received a salary of £1.7 million in the previous year? What should we make of the dot.com millionaires who had made a fortune only to see it collapse in value? How should Christians respond? The media carried images of churches in Birmingham praying for the future of Longbridge and ministering to those affected. The Rev. Michael Davies from Lindfield, West Sussex, spoke out against the closures, saying 'This has led to the destruction of rural communities and for many old people it's a disaster'.[5]

The Archbishop of Canterbury, George Carey, warned in his Easter Day sermon in Canterbury Cathedral against the glitter of dot.com society.[6] Yet there is a danger in all this. Christians complain of their caricatured image in the media; business is no less caricatured.[7]

There is no easy answer to Rover, bank branch closures or to the dot.coms. What this chapter will aim to do is:

- In 'Complexity and Confusion, Critics and Christians', consider the very real problems in building a Christian perspective on business and law and how these can be resolved;
- In 'Committees, Commissions, CLRSG and Company Law', look at the importance of the role of the company director and apply a Christian perspective to the assumptions and values of the law reform process;
- In 'Coming to a Christian Conclusion', reflect on how Christians can move the debate on.

COMPLEXITY AND CONFUSION, CRITICS AND CHRISTIANS

This section identifies three main difficulties to building a Christian perspective on business: the complexity of the law and its evolution; the confusion as to both whether there can be a Christian perspective and if so what it should be; and the competition to a Christian perspective provided by other perspectives.

Complexity of the law and its evolution

The areas of law which have a direct bearing on business are voluminous. Fundamental are core areas of the English legal system generally, contract law and property law, but in addition, there are commercial law, employment law, product liability law, environmental law and taxation. If a business is carried out as a partnership or as a company then partnership law or company law will additionally be relevant. Some businesses will be subject to further regulation because of the particular type of business they conduct, for example, investment businesses are subject to financial services legislation. It will be evident that the question posed as to whether business law is moving away from Judaeo-Christian values is not likely to be a straightforward one to answer.

The complexity of the laws affecting business is a problem in its own right. First, few lawyers now would be likely to claim expertise in all areas of law which might affect a business. This makes it difficult to have an overview of the responsibilities owed by a business. It has been a major weakness in the argument that companies should owe greater responsibilities to employees, consumers and the environment that detailed discussion of actual responsibilities of companies as businesses under specialist areas of legislation has often been lacking. Second, the separate evolution of these areas of law has resulted in each being influenced by different value systems, rendering it overly simplistic to make generalised claims as to the appropriateness of those values. For example, the early development of contract law was based on the notion of 'sanctity of contract', placing a high value on personal autonomy whereas recent developments have been characterised by a more interventionist approach. Employment law has likewise seen a shift in emphasis supplementing a contract-based approach with a rights-based statutory framework capable of embracing changed social values towards gender, race and sexual orientation. The conclusion must be that any Christian perspective must attempt the paradox of both recognising this overall picture while being sufficiently focused to be able to analyse a particular area of law in adequate depth.

Confusion as to a Christian perspective

The complexity of the law regulating business would make the development of a Christian perspective difficult. However, it is made doubly difficult by the confusion that exists. This takes two forms: first, whether a Christian perspective is feasible and/or desirable, and second, what form that perspective should take.

Whether a Christian perspective on business is feasible and/or desirable

There are a variety of objections to a Christian perspective on business.

Christian principles on business cannot be derived from the Bible

The economist, Donald Hay, in setting out the basis for his own theological ethics, in *Economics Today: A Christian Critique*,[8] identifies and discusses three objections which emerge from theological writing to the derivation of principles of biblical social ethics generally from Scripture. These are: (1) that social principles cannot be derived from Scripture; (2) that Scripture should be applied directly; and (3) the use of the New Testament is inappropriate. The arguments presented by Hay can, perhaps, be clarified by recasting his analysis by reference to objections to the Old and New Testaments respectively. The arguments against reliance upon the Old Testament appear to be: (1) it can only be understood in context, ie of salvation in the Exodus and the lack of distinction between church and state in ancient Israel; (2) it is rendered irrelevant because of cultural distance, ie rules for a primitive society can have no relevance to a modern society; (3) the New Testament does not encourage the application of the Old Testament to society; (4) the Old Testament rules are superseded by the New Testament; and (5) the process of deriving principles from the Old Testament is fallible. The arguments against reliance on the New Testament appear to be: (1) it must likewise be interpreted in context, here an eschatological context; (2) its application is for Christians and therefore neglects questions of sin, salvation and judgement. Hay presents a range of answers to these objections. At the risk of oversimplification, the core of these is that in the mind of God there must be principles for social and economic life and that it would be strange if God's revelation was such that these principles could not be discoverable or if these principles were inconsistent and therefore the implied disjunction between Old Testament and New Testament ethics is given too much weight.

I would entirely concur with this. In my view, the objections essentially relate to three core issues: (1) authority, which goes to utility; (2) context, which affects interpretation and relevance; and (3) process, which is fallible because of the two opposed positions of literalism or subjectivity. Ultimately, the answer to (1) and (2) is related to belief and faith: the Christian believes in the Bible as God's revelation and therefore that this revelation has a purpose and value. In terms of (2) and (3) it is interesting to observe that lawyers who are continually involved in the interpretation of legal texts, whether judicial or legislative, have developed a range of principles to assist them, not least where existing rules are silent, unclear or produce an absurd result. Such rules govern for example when it is appropriate for a literal construction to be adopted and when it is appropriate for regard to be had to underlying principles and so on. However, perhaps more fundamental is that the debate on context often surrounds questions such as usury where the issues are genuinely complex (though not insoluble). What is striking about this debate is that there are a whole range of biblical principles which are relatively sparsely discussed perhaps because they appear obvious, self-evident. Basics such as Leviticus 19:11–12, 'Do not steal. Do not lie. Do not deceive one another', on which much of business depends, are often under-emphasised. Even here there is a tendency for ethicists to find hard cases to argue for the disapplication of the principles. Yet lawyers have long held that hard cases make bad law.

Christianity is concerned with the spiritual

The business ethicist, Elaine Sternberg, is well known for her publication *Just Business*.[9] She states this to be a systematic, reasoned argument about what constitutes ethical conduct for business and distinct from those argued to apply incoherent philosophical doctrines to misunderstood business practice.[10] In Sternberg's view much of the 'sanctimonious' criticisms of business that pass as business ethics deserve to be dismissed.[11] The philosophical basis for the book appears to be based on Aristotle.[12] One of the main arguments in the book is that its Ethical Decision Model can provide a general framework for resolving questions of business ethics.[13] In Sternberg's view the purpose of business is the maximisation of owner value over the long term by selling goods or services[14] while satisfying the requirements of ordinary decency and distributive justice.[15] Ordinary decency is stated to comprise two principles: fairness and honesty. Fairness includes organisational rules that are applied systematically and even-handedly and honouring agreements, while honesty means telling the truth.[16] It excludes lying, cheating, stealing, killing coercion, physical violence and illegality.[17] The basis for these is stated to be that they 'are simply wrong'.[18] Distributive justice is interpreted as meaning that organisational rewards should be proportional to contributions made to organisational ends.[19]

To be fair, Sternberg recognises the need for ethical constraints on business: she returns to this in detail in the last chapter of her book, 'Morals and markets'.[20] First, she argues that such questions are not questions of business ethics. Giving examples of tobacco and pornography, she concludes that the test is simply whether the company is maximising long-term owner value. Giving examples of contract killing and slavery, she argues that these are incompatible with ordinary decency. So where might one ask is the place of Christianity in this? Sternberg acknowledges[21] that there are apparent similarities in the sense that the same conduct may be specified from both an ethical and a religious perspective, and religion may have an effect on business; for example, religious principles might rule out a particular business sector. However, she argues that religion cannot alter the purpose of business or what counts as proper business conduct. In effect business is an autonomous concept. Religion is seen as distinctive because of its otherworldly focus, its connection with the divine, or with the saving of souls. To the extent that it moves away from this it is seen as difficult to distinguish from a social welfare movement. Insofar as religion prescribes other values than long-term owner value it is not providing ethical direction for business but something other than business.

It would be outside the scope of this chapter to attempt a full criticism of Sternberg's arguments. However, the following points merit consideration. First, it is submitted that the apparent similarities involve the greatest degree of divergence. The concern of Christian theology with conduct derives from an entirely different ideological framework to that of ethical philosophy and cannot be separated from the totality of that. In particular, I am left unconvinced by her principle of ordinary decency and what there is to underpin it. Why should anyone care? Presumably the ethically disposed might care, but from a Christian perspective mankind is inherently sinful, and much present ethical concern might be argued to be attempting to fill the ethical hole left in a post-Christian generation. Second, while Christianity undoubtedly has a connection with the divine, it is or at least should not be otherworldly or concerned simply with the saving of souls. Indeed, it is at the root of Christianity that Christians are to be in the world not taken out of it; that Christians are to be the salt of the world; that religious leaders were condemned precisely because they were more concerned with otherworldliness than issues of justice. Third, the argument that insofar as Christianity is concerned to set other objects for business then the result is something other than business appears to be semantic. Yet many of the established boundaries of business resulted from Christian social reform: consider the abolition of slavery; the prevention of child exploitation. All these issues involved a restriction on the maximisation of long-term owner value.

In fact, a very different argument can be put forward and has been by Bill Maughan and myself.[22] This is that there is a logical link between the Mosaic biblical laws and economic efficiency. Economics developed from inductive and deductive observations of those early market economies and led to the formulation of the economic model and to the development of the modern concept of economic efficiency. Our research has demonstrated that there is evidence of considerable congruence between the legal environment required to promote economic efficiency and the Mosaic biblical laws that have been influential on many legal systems throughout the world. Accordingly, I would reject Sternberg's approach, instead arguing that it is in fact Judaeo-Christian values which have played a vital role in establishing the conditions in which economic efficiency is possible. A rejection of those values could in fact place economic efficiency at risk.

A response based on principle, precedent and pragmatism

The approach taken in this chapter is a modified version of principles put forward by the author in a paper presented to the Lawyers' Christian Fellowship Academic Conference in 1996 on 'A Christian Vision for Corporate Governance'.[23] The justification for a Christian perspective on business arises from three sources: principle; precedent and pragmatism, which, of course, overlap. The argument based on principle was that Christian theology encompasses business. The Old Testament contains an entire code of social regulation, some of which prescribed the general conditions necessary for business activity, for example, rules relating to integrity, such as the prohibitions on lying and theft and specific conditions, such as rules governing weights and measures and the charging of interest. The New Testament assumed much of this general social framework and extended it. The argument based on precedent was that Christian theology has traditionally been applied to business. It drew attention to the wide variety of theological reflection and influence on business throughout history until the present day across major denominations. It is important not to neglect this influence which has operated both to set the limits on unacceptable business behaviour as well as providing innovative models of good business practice. The argument based on pragmatism was that Christian theology has a unique role to play in the debate. This stressed how Christians could be regarded as stakeholders in corporate society and the need for Christian activism based on: (1) the spiritual significance of the powers vested in corporations; (2) the concern for justice and the victims of injustice; (3) the value base offered which is lacking from the secular framework.

What form a Christian perspective on business should take

Many Christians and Christian organisations have sought to identify the form that a Christian perspective on business should take. The common feature of much of this work is that it has taken place at a very high level of generality. Typically, the focus has been on the purpose of business, the place of competitive markets and distributional issues. By and large the literature is focusing on a 'given' something which it is difficult if not impossible to envisage changing, not least because, much as many may wish to move away from the present economic model, no-one has yet been able to come up with an alternative that does not involve coercion and in a globalised world a global government. As will be readily appreciated in even the most basic form of society trade will be desirable and this can only be based on exchange, gift or compulsion. Accordingly, much of this literature fails to address real-world issues of present rather than hypothetical concern.

Nonetheless, there are a number of publications worthy of merit, and to which further reference shall be made. Donald Hay has written a highly effective Christian critique of economics in *Economics Today*,[24] particularly valuable for its attention to methodological rigour. *A Christian Social Perspective*[25] by Alan Storkey is valuable for its sociological insights. Richard Higginson provides a contribution in the field of business ethics with *Called to Account*[26] and to management theory with *Transforming Leadership*.[27] Michael Schluter and David Lee provide an interesting alternative 'relational' approach in *The R Factor*.[28] Russell Sparkes provided an in-depth analysis of ethical investment in The *Ethical Investor*.[29] There are a number of thought-provoking essays published by Grove.[30] The papers from the annual academic conference of the Lawyers' Christian Fellowship have been published and form a growing resource of Christian perspectives on legal issues, including business.[31] Clearly such a list is not comprehensive but it does indicate the variety of business issues which have received in-depth scrutiny from a Christian perspective.

Among such a volume of resources from such a variety of disciplinary backgrounds is it possible then to discern any dominant theme? Any organising principle? The following appear to be commonly adopted approaches:

Stewardship

The concept of stewardship pervades much Christian writing. Donald Hay relies extensively on it in a closely argued series of biblical principles for economic life. Eight principles are set out to govern the ideal economy yet he is realistic to add a separate section which asks what allowance should be made for the sinfulness of man.[32] Hay defines the concept of stewardship in this way. The idea reminds us that our personal talents and abilities and the natural resources with which we work are God's provision for us. They are not our personal possessions but are entrusted to us. Therefore, we must account to God for the use made of them. The principles derived from this are grouped into three categories: (1) creation and man's dominion; (2) man and his work; (3) distribution of goods. The detailed principles contain a mixture of rights and responsibilities. Man has rights to: use creation to provide for his existence; work; access to resources; basic needs of food, clothing and shelter. The responsibilities are: not to waste or destroy the created order; to exercise stewardship of resources and talents; to determine the disposition of resources; to work; not to consume the entire product of resources so that the rich should help the poor. These principles are well thought-out and supported. However, they are not necessarily straightforward to rely upon for detailed policy development.

Relationships and community

The importance of relationships and community are the focus of many writers. Michael Schluter and the Cambridge-based Relationships Foundation have done much to promote this concept and to build strategic alliances at a secular level which share this value. Michael Schluter and David Lee take as their goal the need to improve the quality (ie the closeness) of social relationships and to create public policy accordingly. They argue[33] for a concept of 'relational proximity' involving five factors: 'directness' ie quality of communication; 'continuity' ie frequency, regularity and amount of contact, and length of relationship; "multiplexity" ie variety of contexts of meetings; 'parity' ie mutual respect and fairness in the relationship; and 'commonality' ie shared goals, values and experience. The criteria are based on Christian assumptions about human beings and have proven a useful approach to the practical application of Christian principles, not least because of the objective method they provide to analyse situations and act in effect as an audit tool.

Justice and the kingdom of God

This approach is most closely associated with liberation theology.[34] The form of analysis adopted is heavily influenced by Marxism and is consequently critical of, or hostile to, capitalism, and is therefore not considered further in this chapter.

A composite approach?

A number of Christian writers, instead of focusing on a dominant theme, have isolated a range of principles, including those set out above. A good example of this is Alan Storkey who identifies nine principles,[35] including not only stewardship but also economic blessing, economic judgement and economic fairness. Similarly Richard Higginson stressed the need to make imaginative connections so as to formulate metaphors, draw analogies and make connections to bridge the gap between the Bible and the modern world.[36] Indeed, these approaches were essentially similar to those taken in 'A Christian Vision for Corporate Governance' by the author. This approach distinguished two basic types of biblical principle relevant to corporate governance – or business; those which dealt with the *nature* of humanity and those which dealt with the *purpose* of humanity. I will apologise here to my economist friends because I will be taking a substantial liberty with their approach. This is to label these principles as positive and normative – 'is' and 'ought' principles. I will refer to them as a model insofar as they represent a simplified approach to reality:[37] a few short principles cannot attempt to sum up the doctrinal richness of Christianity. Yet models prove useful in many disciplines.

A positive model?

The positive model provided by Christianity (which I will refer to in this chapter as 'the Christian positive model') lies in its ability to explain and therefore in some measure to predict reality. There are difficulties in attempting this, not least because the Christian perspective on the world is now so different from the secular. In fact many otherwise reasonable people have very strange world-views compared to the Christian! After all, Christianity stands or falls on the historicity of the resurrection of Jesus Christ.[38] The two principles identified in 'A Christian Vision for Corporate Governance' were that: (1) people are inherently unethical (for which I believe I would now prefer to substitute 'sinful'); and (2) people are of value.[39] Both principles require considerable expansion to be of use. A third might have been added that 'people are aware of God's requirements through conscience and the natural order'.[40] Perhaps more controversially a fourth might tentatively be added that organisations and structures based on or pervaded by sin will, in the long term, fail. Such an approach might well be illustrated by the former Soviet Union which was built on sin on a pervasive basis: it was truly an 'evil Empire'. At its most totalitarian it seemed impervious to external forces of right and decency. A Christian analysis would predict that the Soviet Union would fall in the long run. The same might be predicted of any company or other organisation whose governance is pervaded or affected by sin: hence the relevance of Christianity as an explanatory and predictive tool in the context of business. Indeed, it is interesting to speculate whether some major corporate scandals, such as the collapses of Robert Maxwell's empire or BCCI might have been predicted from a Christian perspective. Interestingly, a survey of the top 500 American corporations showed that two-thirds listed in 1956 had disappeared and that only twenty-nine of the biggest one hundred were still there a working life later, and noted that the survivors were those with a strong moral core.[41] Equally care must be taken when making assumptions in this area. A 1999 comparison[42] of the top ten UK unit trusts with the top ten ethical funds compared how £1000 invested in September 1994 in Sovereign Ethical would then have been worth £2031, but if in Aberdeen Technology £5004. Food for thought.

A normative model?

The normative model provided by Christianity (which I will refer to in this chapter as 'the Christian normative model') can be derived from its guidance on human conduct. Again, a simplified approach is taken. The principles adopted in 'A Christian Vision for Corporate Governance' were that: (1) people are intended to live in relationship with God and each other; (2) people are trustees and managers of God's creation; and (3) people should receive and deliver justice.

The first principle focuses on the purpose of much Christian theology: the importance of relationships. The theological basis for this is the Christian doctrine of love. The emphasis is on relationships both between people and God. Michael Schluter and David Lee have summarised their presuppositions for relationism as being: the intrinsic value of all human life; the primary importance of good interpersonal relationships to both individual and societal well-being; the dependency on the presence of obligation and choice in the social structure for good relationships; and the understanding that a good relationship is primarily a morally good relationship.[43] I have termed this last presupposition elsewhere 'relational integrity'[44] and attempted to develop this concept further. It is relational integrity that provides a justification for laws which deal with the consequences of non-relational conduct such as lying, deceiving and stealing, which are so important in a business context. It also serves to distinguish secular notions of good relationships which can amount to no more than cronyism from the Christian notion of a morally good relationship.

The second principle focuses on the words trustees and managers have chosen to deliberately avoid the language of stewardship. The reason for this is that I am unconvinced by the argument that stewardship should be an organising principle for business. A phrase which has been recently adopted[45] in the context of company law reform is that of the 'responsible risk-taker' and, at the risk of following fashion, this might be clearer again. The ordinary meaning of stewardship is unexceptional: the Concise Oxford Dictionary[46] defines it as 'person entrusted with management of another's property', in a sense the archetypal definition of a director's role. Yet it says nothing about the purpose of that entrustment. The oft unspoken assumption is that stewardship is a role analogous to that of a museum curator, there to preserve property intact for visitors: exactly the image Jesus criticised in the parable of the 'talents'.[47] In other words it is a largely passive role: there is no competition, no innovation, nothing that involves a smidgeon of risk. Yet competition, innovation and risk are exactly what those involved in business are engaged in. The constant imagery of stewardship somehow implies that these are wrong, tainted with greed perhaps. Yet there is little evidence to support that from a theological perspective. Most often cited is Genesis 1:28 that man should be fruitful, increase in number, fill the earth and subdue it; to rule over the animal kingdom. This arguably supports the opposite of the proposition advanced for it. In fact it is strongly arguable that it has only been through competition, innovation and risk that man has been able to carry out the injunction in Genesis. Ponder the prediction of the economist, Thomas Malthus (1766–1834), who predicted that continued population growth was unsustainable.[48] People generally invest expecting a company to be competitive, innovative and risk-taking. Another way of making the same point is to consider the opposite of these characteristics. A business which is not subjected to competition will tend not to take risks or innovate; rather than serving society it is likely to abuse society in the shape of its shareholders who will receive an inadequate return, consumers who will pay over-the-top prices for a poor product and perhaps the environment which may be damaged to boot.[49] In conclusion, these principles form the justification for laws helping people to enter business and protecting them from the worst consequences of failure while regulating those who abuse this.

The third principle focuses on justice. Writers on Christian ethics have observed that there has been a change in emphasis from a theology of the kingdom – in which justice would play a key part – to a theology of love. It is submitted that the definition of love adopted above enables these principles to be reconciled. We have already seen that from a Christian perspective a good relationship is a morally good relationship. Christians should therefore reject any secular notion that love and relationships justify the abandonment of justice: a failure to adhere to principles of justice is probably one of the least loving things that can be done and one which is likely to lead to bad relationships. Often the language of love and relationships appears to be used in a secular context as a mere façade, obscuring or avoiding questions of right and wrong. Love and relationships cannot be built on a foundation of lies, cheating, or stealing.

Competition with other perspectives

This chapter is concerned with business law. It is important to be aware of the sea change which has taken place over the last two decades or so in the academic study of law. The most common approach was what is commonly referred to as 'black letter' or 'doctrinal' law. Kevin McGuinness has described this as 'largely deductive in approach: basic rules of law are stated as axioms, one reasons out the result, testing the broad probability of each particular outcome among a range of possible outcomes against an extensive database of previously decided cases'.[50] It is concerned substantially with finding out what the law *is* and applying this to particular factual situations; in this sense it has been client-orientated: to enable a client to be advised how a particular problem is likely to be determined by a court. This is a positive use of law. However, lawyers have great difficulty when it comes to the normative aspects of their discipline: what *ought* the law to be. Traditionally their training has enabled them to bring little to the table on this: a collection of legal maxims built up from a study of decided cases, such as the need for legal certainty or hard cases make bad law. When pressed resort is made to educated common sense, perhaps informed by Christian[51] (when Christian beliefs were more widespread) or political beliefs.[52] This has proven inadequate when major reviews of law have taken place and law reform has to be justified from first principles. The response has been the development of what might be termed 'perspective analysis'. One example of this, 'law and economics', has featured in the Law Commission's recent work on directors' duties, considered further below.

There are a wide range of types of perspective analysis which are contributing to the law reform debates. These include 'law and economics', 'sociological', 'critical legal studies', 'feminist', 'gay and lesbian'. Most make some claim to a scientific basis, but arguably most are dominated by ideology. Many of these perspectives are promoted by access to a specialised journal published by a mainstream publisher, or receive an airing in mainstream journals. What is often noticeably lacking from either are religious perspectives, whether Christian, Islamic, Jewish or other, notwithstanding the considerable insights which might be provided. There is little point in seeking to speculate as to the reasons for this save to observe that the consequences for influencing the direction of debate are grave. Unless Christians make their voice heard they will undoubtedly not get the laws in business – or elsewhere – they would prefer.

Not only is Christianity in competition with other perspectives but it is also potentially unwelcome. In a post-Christian era although many continue to adhere to Christian values without being aware of their source, many do recognise and reject them without compunction. Indeed, Christian values in the area of sexual morality are often derided, particularly through the media. It comes as no surprise then that Christians increasingly discover that there is less of a consensus over the seriousness with which other Christian values as basic as those that it is wrong to lie, cheat, or steal should be treated. The causes and solutions of a problem of this magnitude are outside the scope of this chapter but clearly have a bearing upon it.[53] Not least, because of evidence of an apparent preparedness to change Christian values so that they are more acceptable/aligned to societal values. There has, for example, been the undignified sight of the Church of England appearing to negotiate over Section 28. There is no justification for changing Christian ethics just because at a *particular* moment in time in a *particular* country in *particular* circles they happen to be unfashion-able. There is indeed no *power* to change Christian ethics. If Christians depart from Christian ethics, then their views may well be 'the views of a few nice people on matters that will not offend anyone' but they will not be Christian ethics. The time to fight for Christian values is not when they are widely accepted but now when they are widely derided and ridiculed.

COMMITTEES, COMMISSIONS, CLRSG AND COMPANY LAW

This section looks at the importance of the company director and the legal framework for directors' regulation and applies the Christian framework developed above to the values revealed by the reform process.

The importance of the company director

The directors of companies within the United Kingdom are responsible for an astonishing value of business activity. According to a 1998 survey, the total market capitalisation of British public companies amounted to more than £1.5 trillion: only slightly less than the next three nations in Europe (Germany, France and Switzerland) put together; by the same measure, 51 of the world's 500 largest industrial and commercial corporations were British.[54] Yet even smaller companies are important in terms of economic activity. A 1997 survey indicated that at least 99 per cent of businesses in all but a handful of industry sectors were small- or medium-sized companies and that small companies accounted for 45 per cent of non-Government employment.[55]

The role of directors is central to this. According to Table A,[56] the statutory model constitution for companies, 'the business of the company shall be man-aged by the directors who may exercise all the powers of the company'. The Cadbury Committee has described[57] the system of corporate governance in these terms:

Boards of directors are responsible for the governance of their com-panies. The shareholders' role in governance is to appoint the directors and to satisfy themselves that an appropriate governance structure is in place. The role of the auditors is to provide the shareholders with an external and objective check on the directors' financial statements.

The Hampel Committee endorsed[58] the Cadbury Committee's definition, observing that 'it puts the directors of a company at the centre of any discussion on corporate governance'. Nonetheless, it is important not to overstate the position. In the case of large listed companies, it tends to assume that the ownership of a company's shares is dispersed and therefore that control of the company has separated, passing into the hands of directors. This proposition may be weakened due to greater institutional shareholding and activism. In the case of small unlisted companies, the position is qualified by the fact that directors will often be substantial shareholders as well. However, while the role that shareholders and others play, and might play, must not be neglected, that of directors remains central.

The current legal framework outlined

The legal context for directors' duties is found within company law.[59] Company law is the body of law broadly concerned with the formation, administration and winding up of companies; it establishes the powers and duties of those involved in company governance; it establishes protection for certain categories of person with a financial interest in them, most significantly shareholders and creditors. The law is primarily statutory having evolved from the earliest modern companies' legislation which originated between 1845 and 1862 and has been subject to reform/consolidation on approximately twenty-year intervals until the 1960s. The law is bulky and complex: the current edition of CCH *British Companies' Legislation* runs to something in the region of 5000 pages. In addition to this, for example, companies listed on the Stock Exchange are governed by additional rules contained in the Yellow Book which place significant additional restrictions on directors' freedom.

The company law regulation of directors' duties is primarily concerned with ensuring the accountability of directors to their company, in general meaning the company as a separate legal entity, and not individual shareholders or other groups. Other areas of the general law, for example, criminal law or taxation law may also expose directors to personal liability, but are outside the scope of this chapter for reasons of space. The legal regulation of directors' duties is also only a small part of the wider framework of company law which ensures the accountability of directors. Examples of that wider framework would include the requirements for company meetings, the disclosure of information as to the company's activities and the power of a majority of a company's members to remove a director. Not least there are the provisions which enable a court to disqualify a director, for example, on the ground of 'unfitness' and that indirectly do so much to establish the boundaries of acceptable directorial conduct. This wider framework is also outside the scope of this chapter for reasons of space. The duties with which we are concerned are those established by the courts and extensively supplemented by Parliament, and which are concerned with the liability of a director to his company where broadly speaking appropriate minimal competence and/or integrity have not been demonstrated. However, in considering the adequacy of these duties it is important to continue to bear in mind the existence of both the general law and the wider framework of company law.

Company law has never set out to prescribe a minimal level of competence for directors by requiring any formal educational qualification, as it has been generally thought undesirable to discourage entrepreneurs from using the corporate form on this account. The courts have likewise traditionally been loath to impose liability for negligence, that is a breach of care and skill although recently changes in insolvency legislation have marked a shift in this, the effect of which is unclear. In contrast, the courts have penalised a lack of integrity quite severely in the form of a conflict of interest, though often the effects of this will be mitigated by a company's constitution where the interest is appropriately disclosed. Parliament has intervened with what is now *Part X of the Companies Act 1985* to supplement the judicial position with rules of labyrinthine complexity, covering a wide range of general and specific issues. The most important general rules relate to a director's disclosure of interests to the board, substantial property transactions involving a director or persons connected with him or loans and similar transactions concerning a director. There has been a broad consensus that the law in this area merits reform, though little consensus as to the direction such reform should take.

The problem: fat cats and all that

Questions of the extent of directors' responsibilities and their actual substance have formed the subject of much of recent debate on the reform of company law and regulation. There have been significant initiatives of a self-regulatory nature, including the Reports of the Cadbury Committee, the Greenbury Study

Group[60] and the Hampel Committee, the 'corporate governance committees'.[61] There has also been a near constant stream of output from government bodies, including the Report of the Law Commissions, rather inelegantly entitled *Company Directors: Regulating Conflicts of Interests and Formulating a Statement of Duties*;[62] the work of the Company Law Review Steering Group under the auspices of the Department of Trade and Industry ('the CLRSG'), in particular, the Modern Company Law Review Consultation Documents on *The Strategic Framework*[63] and *Developing the Framework*[64] as well as a Consultation Document on Directors' Remuneration issued by the DTI.[65]

Why is all this attention being paid to directors' duties?[66]

Criticisms of directors' conduct

The official reason for establishing the Cadbury Committee was concern over the perceived low level of confidence both in financial reporting and the ability of auditors to provide safeguards, heightened by some unexpected failures of major companies and criticisms of the lack of effective board accountability for matters such as directors' pay. Specific mention of BCCI and Maxwell in the Report emphasised the role of corporate scandal.[67] Concern over levels of directors' remuneration, already identified as a contributory factor in the establishment of the Cadbury Committee, led to the establishment of the Greenbury Study Group.[68] In particular, the Report of this Group emphasised its origin in large pay increases and large gains from share options in the then recently privatised utility companies sometimes combined with staff reductions, pay restraint for other staff and price increases.[69] Directors' pay was additionally mentioned in the DTI's *White Paper* as a controversial issue contributing to the need for the Modern Company Law Review.[70]

There are, however, no signs of corporate scandals abating. To mention three further scandals reported last year at random: British Biotech; Versailles Group; Wickes. The British Biotech issue involved allegations that the company had made materially misleading statements about its cancer treatment in June 1999.[71] The Versailles Group issue involved allegations of accounting irregularities in relation to FRS 5, the accounting rule governing off-balance-sheet financing.[72] Wickes involved allegations of fraudulent trading and making false statements by former executives.[73] Likewise concerns over directors' remuneration levels continue. A TU report in 1997[74] found that boardroom pay awards were sixteen times those for employees. An IDS report[75] in 1999 showed that increases in executive pay were four times the average rate of increase; chief executives of FTSE 100 companies' remuneration rose by an average 17.6 per cent in the previous financial year. The situation involving the Granada group[76] involved an interesting debate over what was referred to as unprecedented shareholder opposition to the payment at Granada of £375,000 to directors for reduced service contracts. Nineteen per cent of shareholders voting by proxy opposed the retention of a member of the group's remuneration committee and 12 per cent abstained. Yet he was re-elected thanks to 69 per cent of the shares voted. *The Times* observed that if lobbyists could only woo fewer than a fifth of the votes they could hardly claim success and that Granada was hardly an appropriate group to criticise given that profits were rolling in.

Criticisms of directors' accountability

Pressure for reform has also arisen because of intense questioning of the shareholder-orientated structures adopted by countries which adhere to the broad Anglo-American model of the company. This has come from such a variety of perspectives that it is impossible to summarise them here. Internationally, there has been a call for the recognition of 'stakeholder interests', which has been so widely defined that it may include all affected by the actions of companies, including the environment and future generations. David Korten has popularised the argument that the global economic situation is out of control and that radical measures are required to ensure people-centred development, with his book *When Corporations Ruled the World*.[77] In the United Kingdom there has been the debate over industrial democracy associated, for example, with the 1977 Bullock Committee.[78] More recently, John Parkinson has argued for companies to be required to serve the public interest.[79] Saleem Sheikh has argued for companies to assume social responsibilities.[80] Many Christians have argued similarly, see for example, Simon Robinson.[81] There has been a rise in what may be termed 'communitarian' philosophy. All of these suggest that the established goal-posts for director accountability should be widened. There have been relatively few dissenting voices, but prominent among them are the economist Milton Friedman[82] and the business ethicist, Elaine Sternberg.[83] This issue was influential in the establishment of the DTI's

Modern Company Law Review where the duties of directors were lumped together under the heading 'obstacles to progress' and has formed a major theme of both *The Strategic Framework* and *Developing the Framework* Consultation Documents.

Criticism of directors' regulation

Pressure for reform has also arisen because of the complexity and opacity of regulation governing directors itself. This was influential in the involvement of the Law Commission – only its second in company law reform – to review the area with the objectives both of simplifying and modernising the law as well as considering the need for a statutory statement of directors' duties. This problem was also identified by the Modern Company Law Review as an example of over-regulation justifying the instigation of the review.

The solution: back to basics

As we have seen, over the last decade, a number of bodies have examined how directors should be regulated. The extent to which they have gone out of their way to identify the values on which their proposals were, or might have been, based, is significant. This provides a relatively unique opportunity to attempt to gauge the consistency of these values with Christian values. It also poses some difficult problems of methodology. The first relates to identifying values: different bodies use different language with this effect, for example, guiding principles, objectives. The second relates to authenticating these: for example, where values are identified were these actually influential or merely aspirational? The third relates to how these can be evaluated especially when separated from the belief systems which gave rise to them. This part of the chapter is based on: (1) a detailed content analysis of the values of the 'corporate governance committees' based on examining value-laden words in the introductory chapters of their reports;[84] (2) an analysis of the 'guiding principles' and economic analysis of the Law Commission's Consultation Paper and Report on Directors' Duties;[85] and (3) an analysis of the DTI's *White Paper* and appropriate chapters of the CLRSG's consultation documents, *The Strategic Framework* and *Developing the Framework*.[86] The values identified and discussed are grouped for convenience into a number of headings, which inevitably are somewhat subjective: the number of values elicited from the relevant section of the Cadbury Report alone numbered sixty. At each stage the Christian positive and normative models explained above will be applied.

Process and method

There has been a discernible change in the approach to process and method in the development of the various documents. All of the documents were based on extensive *consultation* and involvement of experts. In particular, the CLRSG has published extensive summaries of the responses from consultees.[87] While only detailed analysis would show the extent to which consultation has actually influenced the processes, the commitment to it matters. The work of the corporate governance committees made extensive use of research and experts.[88] The Law Commission's work was most strongly characterised by its heavily methodological approach. While the corporate governance committees had handed down principles, notably the Cadbury Committee, those of openness, accountability and integrity, relatively brief attention was paid to supporting argument.[89] In contrast, the Law Commission went to some lengths to discuss and refine detailed 'guiding principles' as well as to apply 'law and economics' analysis to reform.[90] In addition, the Law Commission commissioned a detailed empirical report to investigate real-life practices to support its work.[91] While much of this has proven controversial there can be little doubt as to the significance of the attempt.[92] Indeed, the CLRSG has gone on since to formulate its own guiding principles and although there is less emphasis on law and economics in the consultation documents it remains visible among influences from a variety of other disciplines.[93]

Applying the Christian positive model, how can the attention to process be explained and what are the likely outcomes from it? Firstly, the extensive processes of consultation reveal the law reform process as incorporating a significant democratic element. It is not my intention here to attempt a Christian critique of democracy, which has been done elsewhere, but simply to apply the simplified model discussed earlier. From this we would see that as a process this has much to commend itself, because it recognises the principle that people are of value and also provides an opportunity for the exercise by them of the principle of conscience. Therefore the process as a process may be commended. However, the substantive outcome of that process has to be considered separately. The principle of man's sinfulness means that a decision taken, even in accordance with a commendable process, may be sinful and therefore be wrong. If this is the case then the principle as to consequence would apply and it would be expected that the outcome would in the long term fail. Accordingly, the democratic nature of the process does not legitimate the end result from a Christian perspective or ensure success. The Christian normative model – to provide guidance on conduct and laws – will be applied separately below to the substantive values indicated. However, it might be observed that in normative terms the process here could be seen as a sign of weakness, the loss of confidence by those responsible for the legislative process as to the ideology or values which should govern reform.

The question of the merit of the use of 'law and economics' analysis also raises issues beyond this chapter. Not least, law and economics possesses its own, highly advanced, positive and normative models. There are aspects of 'law and economics' analysis with which Christians would concur. Economic analysis is concerned with questions such as the allocation of scarce resources which Christians are also concerned with.

Applying the Christian positive model, the fundamental issue is the concept of the 'rational actor' which makes assumptions as to the nature of mankind. For example, Cheffins[94] states 'rational actors, under economic theory, make decisions so as to improve their personal well-being, frequently referred to as their "utility", "welfare" or "wealth"'. Christians are likely to concur with such a description as applicable to mankind's fallen state and therefore as an appropriate assumption for the reform of secular laws but do not see this as the ideal. Christians also make a moral judgement on this approach to motivation on which economic analysis is silent.

Applying the Christian normative model, a problem is posed by the relationship between economic analysis and other values. To what extent should economic efficiency be an important or dominant goal? Dias, the writer on jurisprudence, identified the following values of the common law:[95] national and social safety; sanctity of the person; sanctity of property; social welfare; equality; consistency and fidelity; morality; administrative convenience; and international comity. Economic efficiency would at best fall to be an aspect of social welfare. Since such values largely mirror those found in Christianity the question arises as to what weighting Christians should seek to place on economic efficiency. The present law reform debate has no answer to the problem of weighting other than through democratic processes. A final issue is often referred to as the conflict between efficiency and equity and involves the difficult question of the role and content which justice should play in an economic situation. Christianity has the potential to play a useful role in contributing to the debate in this area insofar as it can provide well-developed insights into the concept of justice. Nonetheless, there is much in common between the normative assumptions of economic analysis and a Christian perspective. Economic analysis involves a concern for the provision of reliable information, the keeping of promises and property rights which Christians would share. Yet Christians are likely to be cautious of the ideological component of economic analysis, not least when as with the work of the Law Commission it is used to determine the boundaries of what conduct should be criminalised.

The role of government and law

A perhaps surprising theme that runs through the documents is an apparently low expectation of what governments and laws can achieve. The Cadbury Committee appeared sceptical as to the ability of any system of control to eliminate the risk of fraud without impeding companies' competitive abilities: perhaps a less surprising conclusion given how keen it was to forestall direct government intervention in a number of corporate governance issues.[96] Equally, the Hampel Committee stressed the inability of government to command prosperity.[97] Such an emphasis was more implied than explicit in the Law Commission's work: the law as facilitator principle stressed that the law should facilitate rather than impede proper business; the appropriate sanctions principle stressed the need for sanctions to be effective and realistic; the 'enough but not excessive' principle counselled against excessive regulation of management and directors freedom to make business decisions.[98] The use of economic analysis in its own right makes assumptions as to the role of the state.[99]

The most significant reservations as to the role of government and law comes from the work of the CLRSG. The initial *White Paper* drew attention to this, harking back to the period before 1855 when a key reason for legislation permitting general limited liability was the incorporation by British businessmen of companies under French and American laws. It emphasised that in a globalised economy company law could not be considered in isolation and must not become a disincentive to establishing in Britain.[100] However, the strongest reservations appear in the CLRSG's *Strategic Framework*. This contained a section devoted to 'The Importance of Change'.[101] The changes considered appear to have been seen as matters where government control was restricted. These changes were: (1) globalisation;[102] (2) Europe;[103] (3) changing patterns of regulation;[104] (4) information technologies;[105] (5) changing patterns of ownership;[106] (6) the modern asset mix[107] and the importance of small and closely held companies.[108] By way of example, the conclusion drawn in respect of globalisation was that if our laws were unduly prescriptive, inflexible, inaccessible or onerous, businesses would choose to incorporate elsewhere.[109] It is perhaps little surprise therefore that one of the three guiding principles of the CLRSG was that of the 'facilitation of transactions – a presumption against prescription'.[110] An example of the impact of globalisation can be seen in *Developing the Framework* where the views of international lawyers to the effect that a move to a pluralist approach would be relatively unattractive to inward investors and those considering establishing businesses in the UK was influential.[111]

From a Christian perspective, the question of the role of government and law are again complex. There are two separate issues which need to be considered. The first is the ability of law to deal with the problems which have caused the debate on directors' duties; the second relates to the changes identified by the CLRSG.

The question of the ability of the law to prevent fraud and fat-cat remuneration raises basic questions for which Christianity has a clear explanation. Applying the Christian positive model, these arise out of one common factor: man's sinful nature. Regulation is unlikely to ever be an adequate way of dealing with this though it can go some way to protecting the vulnerable who might be affected. The outcome in the long term from a Christian perspective, if such problems are not dealt with effectively, may well be organisational failure. Applying the Christian normative model, Christians would seek solutions based on achieving good relationships, responsibility in risk-taking and justice. Such solutions could also draw on specific principles derived from Judaeo-Christian values. For example, these include respect for property; in the context of excessive remuneration the normative solution might therefore be based upon enhancing the rights of the owners, ie shareholders.

The changes identified by the CLRSG are not really issues of values but are essentially presented as a set of factual issues. On the face of it, this could mean that it would be difficult to apply a Christian framework since this would be the equivalent of attempting a Christian perspective upon, for example, the fact that a day has twenty-four hours in it, which is a logical non-sequitur. However, the extent to which these are indeed facts – 'givens' – or man-made constructs should be tested individually; where they are man-made constructs which appear to have harmful consequences then the explanation, applying a Christian positive model, is likely to be based on sin and a normative solution can be constructed accordingly. For example, in constructing a normative solution in the context of globalisation, Christians are concerned with the legitimate exercise of power wherever it is located: the location may be diffuse, as in a democracy or in a global setting, or concentrated, as in a dictatorship.

Business, companies and stakeholders

All the reform bodies have delivered a strong vote of confidence in the basic structures of business, companies and directors. None has felt it necessary to advocate radical change.

All the corporate governance committees emphasised the importance of *business success*, with the Hampel Committee taking the view that business prosperity took priority over accountability or relationships and additionally stressing the need for a long-term view.[112] Yet both Cadbury[113] and Greenbury[114] were haunted by the problems that had given rise to them; Hampel fleetingly referred to the need to avoid disaster and identified the issue of the public acceptability of corporate conduct.[115] The Law Commission's view was that 'the wider context of company law is regulating commercial activity so that it operates efficiently and promotes prosperity'.[116] However, the strongest emphasis of this nature came from the work of the DTI and CLRSG. The title of the *White Paper* which has continued through the Review is *Modern Company Law for a Competitive Economy*, itself making a strong declaration of belief. Margaret Beckett, then Secretary of State for Trade and Industry, stated in the introduction that

Modern companies are one of the key pillars of our approach to competitiveness; and we are determined to ensure that we have a

61

framework of company law which is up to date, competitive and designed for the next century, a framework which facilitates enterprise and promotes transparency and fair dealing.[117]

The Strategic Framework built upon this stating that 'Law for a Competitive Economy' was the 'predominant objective' while also observing that 'this does not mean that the law should merely facilitate and secure freedom for management and controllers of companies. There is a trade-off between freedom and abuse, and between freedom and efficiency'.[118] *Developing the Framework* repeats *The Strategic Framework* in saying that company law should facilitate the exercise of effective business choices so as to maximise wealth and welfare, not only for participants but for all affected by the operation of companies. However, it extends this, arguing that 'in most circumstances the best way of achieving this is to provide the means, and in particular the necessary information, for choices to be exercised and effective commercial relations established in a market economy, without public policy intervention'.[119]

There has been little impetus for changing basic *company structures* given the ringing endorsement of business. This is perhaps surprising given the extensive arguments for two-tier boards, European style, employee or public interest representation on the board and so on. Notwithstanding the problems that led to its creation, the Cadbury Committee stated that the basic framework of corporate governance was sound.[120] The Hampel Committee observed that it had found no support for the import into the UK of a whole system developed elsewhere.[121] The Law Commission commented colourfully in its first Report in the area of company law on Shareholder Remedies that it was concerned not 'to damage the legal skeleton on which the flesh of company affairs is hung',[122] perhaps unfortunately giving the impression that company law looks like a rotting corpse! In its second Report in this area the Law Commission took a conservative approach to the traditional company-law framework, including as guiding principles[123] 'the principle of sanctity of contract', 'a principle of separate but interdependent roles for shareholders and directors'; and 'the commercial judgment principle'. *The Strategic Framework* observed that mandatory requirements to alter board composition would be unlikely to command wide support and the objectives might be achieved in other ways, such as through improved disclosure; even making such change available on an optional basis would not be advocated unless there was strong demand as it would be a major change.[124] Similarly, *Developing the Framework* had reservations about a two-tier board structure on the basis that members of a supervisory board might have a poorer understanding of the business and could not fully perform strategic and relationships roles (in contrast to the use of non-executive directors) and that the legal complexity of permitting two-tier boards was such that, even on an optional basis, they would only be advocated if the merits were very great or they were required by EC law.[125]

The responsibility of directors to *stakeholders* has been a recurring theme motivating reform but has attracted little enthusiasm for change in practice. Little emphasis was placed by the corporate governance committees on the impact of companies on wider communities. The Cadbury Committee observed that financial reporting was important to a wider audience, not least employees;[126] the Greenbury Study Group commented on the effects of directors' remuneration on price increases and employees;[127] the strongest statement was made by the Hampel Committee which stressed the need to develop relationships relevant to the business but equally made clear that this was subject to the overriding objective of the preservation and enhancement of shareholder investment over time'.[128] The Law Commission was prepared to be more flexible, suggesting 'an inclusive principle' that 'the law should permit directors to take into account the interests of persons other than shareholders, to the extent the law allows this'.[129] The DTI's *White Paper*, having identified directors' duties under the heading of 'obstacles to progress', stated that a wider issue for the review should be 'whether directors' duty to act in the interests of their company should be interpreted as meaning simply that they should act in the interests of the shareholders or whether they should also take account of other interests, such as those of employees, creditors, customers, the environment and the wider community'.[130] It questioned 'whether they just represent interesting philosophical ideas and ideals or whether they lead to concrete proposals that should be pursued'.[131] The question was further pursued in *The Strategic Framework*, where the two positions were termed 'enlightened shareholder value' and 'pluralist approaches' respectively.[132] The comparison between these was nonetheless which would best achieve competitiveness and efficient wealth creation while minimising the negative impact of corporate activity.[133] Examples of why the issue was of practical rather than theoretical interest were given as decisions whether to close a plant, with associated redundancies, or to terminate a long-term supply relationship, when continuation would make a negative contribution to shareholder returns:[134] analogous issues to Rover and Barclays identified at the beginning of this chapter.

The latest consultation document, *Developing the Framework*, has explored this further. A pluralist duty was broadly rejected:[135] the reasons are interesting as to the values which prevailed. First, it was stressed that the overwhelming majority of responses opposed change.[136] Second, there were a variety of policy grounds against change: directors would be conferred unpoliceable powers or duties which the courts would have a wide discretion to interpret; the objective might be achieved in other ways; specific legislation applying to all businesses would be preferable; the discipline of the takeover mechanism operating would be prevented; inward investment would be less attractive.[137] Third, there were a range of technical difficulties: it would require competing interests to those of shareholders to be taken into account; constraints on directors under a company's constitution would be affected; change would be inconsistent with the shareholders' power to remove directors; the directors would be in difficulties advising shareholders in takeover situations; finally if wider communities should be taken into account, which ones – overseas communities?[138] While it is not easy to translate these reasons into specific values, the sense is there of a genuine fear of opening Pandora's box, that a core value must be practicality: an ethically attractive proposal in practice becomes one which would confer on directors apparently uncontrolled powers while exposing them to almost unlimited liability to a limitless range of complainants.

Generally, Christian perspectives on *business* have tended to be negative in tenor. This appears to have resulted from a misguided application of the principle of man's sinfulness, which has been adopted as part of the Christian positive model in this chapter. In particular, much of the argument surrounds the New Testament principle that the love of money is the root of all evil. Since money is the motivation for business then business must be especially sinful. Yet it is self-evident that greed is not the only motivator in a business context: many are motivated by notions of job satisfaction – doing a good job – or by providing for their family or by creating something new. Even where there is greed and it leads to scandal this should come as no surprise to a Christian. When did Christians expect mankind to be free of sin? Why should business be free from sin? No other area of life is. Fat cat remuneration issues are being reported in NHS trusts; scandals are being reported in institutions of higher education; sexual scandals have emerged in state care of children which are appalling. In some of these sectors there has even been a 'stakeholder' approach to governance in the sense of attempting to balance a range of stakeholder issues. Business does not have a monopoly on the dark side of human nature. Obviously, the argument that sin is prevalent outside of business does not justify its presence in business. However, it does show that the true problem to be addressed is sin and not business per se. From a Christian perspective, there is no reason why Christians should not share the positive attitude to business which has been shown by the reform bodies.[139] Business does a great deal to ensure that social needs are met. It provides useful work. In fact, the 'caring professions', which it is often felt are more 'Christian' to engage in, are substantially financed through taxes and donations from those working in business.

The application of a Christian positive model to the question of *company structures* initially appears to pose a problem. The principles established earlier are essentially based on the individual, on individual motivation and con-science. How could the question be posed therefore as to whether a company structure could be sinful? The answer would appear to lie in whether the company structures constrain the people who make use of them to act in a sin-ful manner. There are indeed powerful arguments that this is the case: first, that company structures force directors to profit maximise and to restrict forms of profit-sacrificing behaviour; and second, that limited liability, on which most company structures are based, is itself unbiblical, as well as giving rise to relational problems.[140] It would not be possible to consider these arguments fully in this chapter and many Christians may find them persuasive. Yet against these criticisms, there are good reasons why Christians might applaud modern company structures. Evangelical Christians supported the birth of the company in the mid-nineteenth century because the company protected entrepreneurs to some extent from the harsh rigours of bankruptcy if something went wrong.[141] Dealings with limited liability companies, in theory at least, are not compulsory but freely entered into: hence the legal requirement that such associations should include the word 'limited' or appropriate alternatives after their name, rather like a 'red flag' or warning. Furthermore, the law has done much to mitigate the problems of abuse of limited liability.[142] Perhaps more significantly, the company has facilitated the greatest growth in productive co-operative activity that mankind has ever seen, and that emphasis on co-operative relationships arguably outweighs any disadvantage. Not least because the emphasis on productive and co-operative relationships in the context of the progressive globalisation of business does much to strengthen peaceful links between countries and reduce the risk of war.

A Christian perspective on the *stakeholder* issue poses difficulties.[143] The term itself is purely neutral, and was originally used to distinguish the American term 'stockholder' from those without whose support an organisation would cease to exist.[144] Insofar as the term is used in this descriptive fashion, a Christian perspective is not needed. What is more significant is the use of the term in a normative sense: on this basis the interests of stakeholders must be regarded as being of intrinsic value; the term lays the foundation for concepts such as corporate social responsibility.[145] At this stage it becomes relevant to apply a Christian normative model to the concept. At a risk of over-simplification, the result is likely to be that the concept is highly satisfactory from a relational perspective, and in terms of the 'stewardship', 'trusteeship' or 'responsible risk-taker' concepts. However, it would appear to be weaker in terms of justice because it risks infringing the principle of justice which would be strong on the recognition of property rights (unless property rights were themselves redefined).

Competence, integrity and relationships

The Cadbury Committee has earned much praise for its principles of accountability, integrity and openness.[146] The Hampel Committee, however, stressed a range of alternative values, including people, teamwork, leadership, enterprise, experience and skills.[147] Surprisingly, such values did not feature clearly in the Law Commission's guiding principles for the reform of directors' duties: perhaps they were assumed, for example, in the 'appropriate sanctions principle'.[148] *The Strategic Framework* raised under the heading 'freedom and abuse' the need to maintain appropriate high standards of conduct, but the main emphasis was placed upon relationships.[149] It raised a concern that perceptions of shareholder pressures had inhibited long-term investment in value creating internal and external relationships. While not all relationships needed to be co-operative and long-term, very often relationships of this kind were important ingredients of success. Relationships based on mutual trust made it more likely that employees would acquire high levels of skill and knowledge, particularly of a firm-specific kind. The significance of relationships was addressed through the enlightened shareholder value vs pluralist approaches discussed earlier.

The question of competence is interesting in terms of applying the Christian positive model. This has largely focused on sin and therefore might appear to be more concerned with integrity. Could it be said that it is sinful to hold a directorial role while incompetent? First, a person might attain a role which they are not competent to carry out as a result of sin, for example, lying as to their experience or ability. Second, it might be against good conscience to hold on to a role aware of a lack of competence. After all, the effects of incompetent management have potential to spread outwards like ripples in a pond and affect some of the most vulnerable, for example, by leading to shoddy products which harm customers or to redundancies which harm employees. In this sense, competence is no less important than integrity and quite possibly more important. Accordingly, moves to promote competence should be vigorously supported from a Christian perspective.

While it may appear unnecessary to develop a Christian perspective on moves to encourage integrity, the focus can be inadequate, often directed towards independence,[150] whereas the true problem in terms of the Christian positive model is sin, more than a lack of independence. Instead, the focus should be on a fuller concept of integrity of character which encompasses both private and public aspects of life – from a Christian perspective character is indivisible; character flaws that may lead to corporate scandal are rarely likely to be manifested purely in business life. This point merits emphasising; a person who cheats on their husband or wife would seem no less likely to cheat on employees or creditors, for example. Although this risks the accusation that this might lead to a witch hunt, this is now routinely argued whenever any conduct regarded as sin from a Christian perspective is criticised. The result is that sin goes unchallenged and unchecked. If Christians are concerned for the victims of corporate scandals then they must be serious about condemning lack of integrity.

Christians also welcome the focus on relationships, a normative principle which has been identified earlier. However, they often appear from the review process to be a means to an economic end; from a Christian perspective the justification is independent of this. Indeed, the reform process says much about the value of relationships but less as to how they might be measured and encouraged: in contrast, Christians, such as Michael Schluter and the Relationships Foundations are actively engaged in such a process.

Quality of law

Another value which forms a major emphasis of the Law Commission's and the DTI's work is on the quality of the law itself. This has possibly been spurred on by an earlier criticism of the Law Society Company Law Standing Committee which concluded that 'no Government can escape responsibility for the quality of its legislation'.[151] A quarter of the Law Commission's guiding principles encompass this notion: 'a usability principle'; 'a certainty principle'; 'the principle of efficiency and cost-effectiveness'.[152] The DTI *White Paper* also reflected this emphasis, focusing on complexity (arising from over-formal language, excessive detail and over-regulation) and on obsolescent and ineffective provisions.[153] The remaining two of the three guiding principles of *The Strategic Framework* relate to 'accessibility – ease of use and identification of the law' and 'regulatory boundaries – proper jurisdictions'.[154]

Applying the Christian positive model laws are desirable in that mankind is sinful; additionally, good laws have the potential to reinforce conscience. The importance of law is amply demonstrated from the Old Testament where even theological concepts are moulded in legal terms. In the New Testament sin is equated with 'lawlessness' and believers are enjoined to respect the laws of secular rulers. In the light of this it follows that laws should be of the highest quality in their form as well as in their substance, particularly because of the role of conscience. The principles elucidated in the review process are in line with this goal and therefore commend support from Christians. The Christian normative model is inapplicable to this issue which is concerned with the form of laws and not their substance.

COMING TO A CHRISTIAN CONCLUSION

This chapter started with cars, closures and dot.coms, issues of a business nature receiving significant media attention such as the proposed sale of Rover by BMW. A warning was given against making assumptions as to questions of law, Christian ethics and business based on media caricatures. It looked at some of the real difficulties Christians face in building a Christian perspective on these issues: the arguments that a Christian perspective on business is not feasible and/or desirable. In contrast it questioned why anyone should care about some of the alternative foundations offered for business ethics and suggested instead that laws based on biblical foundations might have played a vital role in establishing the conditions in which economic efficiency was possible. It also reviewed some of the arguments as to the appropriate content of a Christian perspective on business: stewardship, relationships and justice. Based on these and other principles, this chapter suggested a potentially powerful approach of creating a Christian positive model and a Christian normative model to apply to business issues. The positive model was based upon a biblical understanding of human nature: simplified here to the notion of man, inherently sinful, yet made in the image of God and of immeasurable value in the eyes of God, possessing a conscience to enable him to distinguish right from wrong. The question was asked as to what extent Christians could use this model as the basis to predict organisational success or failure. The Christian normative model developed the three themes identified into those of good relationships, responsibility in risk-taking, and justice. However, the chapter also noted the increasingly fierce competition that any Christian perspective must face and the growing risk that a Christian perspective will face resistance.

It was on this basis that we looked at the role and importance of the company director and the laws which regulate directorial conduct. We saw how scandals, fat cat remuneration and other issues have led to a range of bodies looking at how directors might be regulated and how evidence of such problems continues to mount. The assumptions and values which formed the basis of the secular response were examined in some detail: issues of process and method, the role of government and law, business, companies and directors, competence, integrity and relationships. Both the Christian positive model and Christian normative model proved effective structures for developing a Christian perspective. First, the importance was shown of being able to separate out policy justifications which are essentially issues of fact – 'givens' – from those which are man-made constructs. One example of this was globalisation. Where a justification is a man-made construct then the motivation behind it can be tested together with its impact. Second, the ideological foundations for reform were found to be wanting: the basis for proposals either not stated, or based on principles underpinned by weak reasoning, or based on economic reasoning. The latter was particularly interesting from a Christian perspective because many of the assumptions made were shared with Christianity yet their goals very different. Third, it was seen how the problems associated with business result from sin but that since all other areas of social activity were also affected by this it could not form a justification for rejection of business: the problem to be remedied was sin. Company structures were examined and it was noted that while there were reasons why Christians might reject the concept of limited liability, company structures as a whole should be applauded for what they had achieved. The 'stakeholding' alternative was considered to have both strong pros and cons from a Christian perspective and therefore other means of achieving what are clearly desirable goals should be found. Fourth, it was argued that incompetence in a director could constitute sin and that moves to encourage directorial competence should have at least an equal priority to issues of integrity and relationships. While moves to encourage integrity in directors should be welcomed it was felt that the emphasis should be broader: Christians do not see integrity as limited to the workplace; in terms of encouraging good relationships Christians had much to offer by way of a constructive contribution to the debate. Finally, although the emphasis on improving the quality of law might appear of limited interest, the emphasis placed by Christians on good conscience meant that the commitment to reform was to be highly commended.

The conclusion from this is that there is indeed a Christian perspective on business, capable of both explaining the problems faced by the reform process and suggesting the basis for effective reform. I have discussed a number of practical reforms, such as social reporting and auditing, greater employee participation and more, in 'A Christian Vision for Corporate Governance', which are consistent with a Christian perspective. The practical issue arises as to what role a Christian perspective has to play in a largely secular society in competition to other perspectives? I believe that the answer is as follows: (1) a Christian perspective on business is based on belief in a Christian world-view derived from the whole of Christian teaching and therefore priority must always be given to introducing people to faith in Christ so that they will share that perspective; (2) a Christian perspective on business places much emphasis on the role of good conscience and therefore a Christian perspective merits promotion on the basis that it will commend itself to those of good conscience; (3) a Christian perspective on business is likely to work and therefore produce successful outcomes for those that follow it and therefore commend itself even to those of bad conscience.

So, in concrete terms, what has a Christian to say about Rover, Barclays, dot.coms and Standard Life? Basically, that Christians believe these events are not simply random happenings in a world out of control; they can be explained from a Christian perspective. More than this, Christians believe that God loves mankind and has revealed to mankind the best way to live and therefore if we follow His way, it is possible to create laws and regulations for business based on good relationships, responsibility in risk-taking, and justice, which should lead to success. Mankind does not need to engage in a guessing game hoping to find the truth.

Notes

1. Stephen Copp is a senior lecturer in law in the School of Finance and Law at Bournemouth University and is associated with the European Centre for Corporate Governance. He has published on corporate governance, company law and contract law, including 'A Christian Vision for Corporate Governance', in *Christian Perspectives on Law Reform*, ed. Beaumont, P. (Carlisle: Paternoster, 1998). He is married to Caroline and has three children, Matthew, Simon and Peter, ranging from seven years to under one year old, and approaches the Christian faith from a charismatic evangelical perspective. Biblical references throughout are to the New International Version, Hodder & Stoughton, 1986. The chapter sets out the position as at 27 April 2000, the date of the lecture.
2. Baldwin, T., 'Alchemy exploits Byers feud with DTI officials', *Times*, 26 April 2000.
3. See Dunne, H., 'Sorry says Middleton as Barclays defends cull', *Times*, 27 April 2000.
4. See English, S., 'Standard Life float goes to vote', *Daily Telegraph*, 26 April 2000.
5. See Dunne, H., op. cit.
6. Bonthrone, P. J., 'Wear Cross with pride, Carey urges Christians', *Telegraph*, 24 April 2000.
7. One valuable exception to this is the film *Other People's Money*, which *inter alia* starred Gregory Peck and Danny de Vito. Using the medium of a debate at the annual stockholder's meeting, such issues were considered with exceptional clarity, placing the responsibility for the particular proposed closure firmly on new technology and the need to attract and reward capital.
8. Apollos, 1989, Chapter 3.
9. Warner, 1994.
10. Ibid., p. 2.
11. Ibid., p. 21.
12. Ibid., p. 3, fn. 5.
13. Ibid., p. 8.
14. Ibid., p. 32.
15. Ibid., pp. 79–80.
16. Ibid., p. 84; respect for property rights which might have been expected to come under this heading is regarded as implicit in the owner principle.
17. Ibid., p. 79.
18. Ibid., p. 77.
19. Ibid., p. 80.
20. Ibid., pp. 251–68.
21. Ibid., pp. 71–2. Her discussion is by reference to 'religion' and not specifically to Christianity, though there is specific reference to the Christian tradition in a subsequent section on suffering and sacrifice, p. 72.
22. Maughan, C. W. and Copp, S. F., 'Economic Efficiency, The Role of the Law, and the Old Testament',

a paper delivered to the Biblical Economics Conference at the Hebrew University of Jerusalem, Israel, 4–7 June 2000.

23. Published in *Christian Perspectives on Law Reform,* ed. Beaumont, P. (Paternoster, 1998), Chapter 5.
24. Op. cit.
25. IVP, 1979.
26. Eagle, 1993.
27. SPCK, 1996.
28. Hodder & Stoughton, 1993.
29. HarperCollins, 1995.
30. For example, Robinson, S., 'Serving Society: The Social Responsibility of Business', *Grove Ethical Studies* No. 86 (Grove, 1992).
31. See *Christian Perspectives on Law Reform,* op. cit., and *Christian Perspectives on Human Rights and Legal Philosophy,* ed. Beaumont, P. (Paternoster, 1998).
32. Op. cit., pp. 70–89.
33. Op. cit., Chapter 3.
34. See, for example, McGrath, A. E., *Christian Theology, An Introduction* (Blackwell, 1996), pp. 105–7; Miranda, J. P., *Marx and the Bible, A Critique of the Philosophy of Oppression* (SCM, 1977) and Bonino, J. M., *Christians and Marxists, the Mutual Challenge to Revolution* (Hodder & Stoughton, 1976).
35. Op. cit., Chapter 14.
36. Op. cit., Chapter 2.
37. A more complex model then might seek to take into account matters such as the continuing supernatural involvement of God in His world, the ultimate finality of the world and judgement and so forth. Nonetheless, it is submitted that the principles set out below are adequate for application in a business environment and as a basis for future, more detailed consideration and expansion.
38. 1 Corinthians 15:13–14.
39. Op. cit., pp. 138–9.
40. Based in part on Romans 1:20.
41. Smythe, Dorward and Reback, *Corporate Reputation: Managing the New Strategic Asset* (Century, 1993) cited by R. Sparkes, op. cit.
42. Daily Telegraph, 2 October 1999, 'The price of conscience'. The question raised by such comparisons might well be the extent to which the concerns of ethical investment coincide with those of Christians, and given the diverse range of Christian beliefs, *which* Christians.
43. See Schluter, M. and Lee, D., op. cit., p. 267.
44. See Copp, S. F., 'Developing a Relationally Based Law of Contract – A Question of Good Faith' (due for publication in *Christian Perspectives on Relationism,* ed. Beaumont, P., Paternoster, 2000).
45. Speech by Stephen Byers, Secretary of State for Trade and Industry, cited in 'Byers to protect enterprise culture' (1999) 20 *The Company Lawyer* 119.
46. Oxford University Press, 1976.
47. Luke 19:11–27.
48. See Galbraith, J. K., *A History of Economics* (London: Hamish Hamilton, 1987), pp. 77–9.
49. For a Christian perspective on competition see Higginson, R., 'The Ethics of Business Competition', Grove Ethical Studies No. 105 (Grove, 1997).
50. 'Research and Research Methodology – An Overview', an unpublished paper delivered at Bournemouth University, 8 October 1996, p. 13: see further 'Law and Economics – a reply to Sir Anthony Mason, C. J. Aust.' (1994) 1 *Deakin L.Rev.* 117.
51. See, for example, Lord Denning M. R., *The Influence of Religion on Law* (Gwent: The Starling Press Ltd, 1989).
52. See, for example, Griffiths, J., *The Politics of the Judiciary* (Font, 1991).
53. The significance of the point has been well emphasised by John Montgomery in 'Why a Christian Philosophy of Law?' in *Christian Perspectives on Human Rights and Legal Philosophy,* ed. Beaumont, P. R. (Paternoster, 1998), p. 73.
54. See McGuinness, K. and Copp, S. F., *The reform of company law: a search for guiding principles,* Chartered Secretary, May 1998, 30 at 31.
55. Company Law Steering Group consultation document, Modern Company Law For a Competitive Economy, The Strategic Framework (DTI, 1999), p. 56, citing the Small and Medium Enterprise (SME) Statistics for the United Kingdom, 1997 (DTI, 1998: URN 98/92).
56. Companies (Tables A to F) Regulations 1985, S. I. 1985/805, Reg. 70. This is subject to the provisions of the Companies Acts 1985–1989, the Memorandum and Articles of Association of the company, and any directions given by special resolution by members. In practice, the most important of these are the extensive powers reserved to members on important issues, such as the power to change the company's Articles of Association under s. 9, Companies Act 1985.

57. Report of the Committee on the Financial Aspects of Corporate Governance (London: Gee & Co, 1992), para. 2.5, see further fn. 62 post.
58. Report of the Committee on Corporate Governance (London: Gee & Co, 1998), para. 1.15, see further fn. 62 post.
59. Detailed references are not set out for this section as the points are made in very general terms only and would require much expansion and qualification; however, a general account of the relevant issues can be found in a number of standard company law texts: a useful and very up-to-date introduction is provided by Griffin, S., *Company Law, Fundamental Principles* (Longman, 2000), especially chapters 16–21.
60. *Directors' Remuneration* (London: Gee & Co, 1995).
61. These bodies were set up, in effect, by City institutions rather than the government and therefore technically their views do not represent government policy. The Committee on the Financial Aspects of Corporate Governance was set up in May 1991 by the Financial Reporting Council, the London Stock Exchange and the accountancy profession, under the chairmanship of Sir Adrian Cadbury (hence it is usually referred to as 'the Cadbury Committee') and reported in December 1992. Although its terms of reference were limited to financial reporting and accountability, in practice, its recommendations impacted on corporate governance more generally. The Study Group on Directors' Remuneration was set up on the initiative of the CBI in January 1995 under the chairmanship of Sir Richard Greenbury (hence it is known as 'the Greenbury Committee') to consider directors' remuneration and reported in July 1995. The Committee on Corporate Governance was established under the chairmanship of Sir Ronnie Hampel (hence it is known as 'the Hampel Committee') to review the code of practice issued by the Cadbury Committee and produced its final report in January 1998. The Hampel Committee subsequently gave rise to a 'Combined Code' derived from all these reports which is now contained in the London Stock Exchange's Yellow Book and is therefore applicable to listed companies. Strictly speaking the reports of the corporate governance committees cannot be considered as those of law reform bodies but have been included because of their close nexus with the law reform process.
62. Law Com. No. 261; Scot. Law Com. No. 173. Referred to here as 'Directors' Duties'.
63. DTI 1999, URN 99/654.
64. DTI, 2000, URN 00/656. It should be noted that the CLRSG documents, such as this, stress that they are the work of the Steering Group and do not represent Government policy, see para. 1.9.
65. DTI, 1999, URN 99/923.
66. For a more detailed consideration, see Copp, S. F., op. cit., pp. 108–28.
67. Op. cit., p. 9.
68. Op. cit., p. 7.
69. Op. cit., paras 1.6–1.8.
70. Op. cit., para. 3.7.
71. See, for example, Commentary, 'Biotech board failure', *Times*, 25 June 1999.
72. See Merrell, C., 'Sky was the limit for the man behind Versailles', *Times*, 10 December 1999. See further Doran, J., 'Investors to seek £23 million from Versailles directors', *Times*, 26 April 2000.
73. See Cunningham, S., 'Four former Wickes directors charged after SFO inquiry', *Times*, 27 May 1999.
74. See Buckley, C., 'Can the global market really justify boardroom excess?', *Times*, 4 August 1999.
75. By Incomes Data Services, an independent research body. See Buckley, C., 'Free-for-all on pay in the boardroom', *Times*, 28 October 1999.
76. Walsh, D., 'Record vote fails to unseat Granada director', *Times*, 5 February 1999 and Commentary, *Times*, 5 February 1999.
77. Earthscan, 1995.
78. Cmnd 6706.
79. Parkinson, J. E., *Corporate Power and Responsibility* (Oxford: Clarendon, 1993).
80. Sheikh, S., *Corporate Social Responsibilities, Law and Practice* (Cavendish, 1996).
81. Op. cit.
82. *The Social Responsibility of Business is to Increase its Profits* (Prentice Hall, 1988), p. 87.
83. Op. cit.
84. Based on an unpublished paper, 'New Frontiers in Governance: An Application of Emerging Principles Beyond Public Companies To Owner-Managed Businesses', delivered by the author at the 1999 Socio-Legal Studies Association Conference, Loughborough University.
85. See further Copp, S. F., 'Company Law Reform: the Legal Framework', *Chartered Secretary*, January 1999, p. 28 and Maughan, B. and Copp, S. F., 'The Law Commission and Economic Methodology: Values, Efficiency and Directors' Duties', (1999) 20 *The Company Lawyer* 109.
86. Op. cit.
87. The influence of consultation can be seen in *Developing the Framework*, op. cit., paras 2.11–2.18, on the issue as to in whose interests the company should be run.

88. See for example Appendix 7 of the *Cadbury Committee Report* setting out details of contributors and similar appendices in the other documents.
89. Op. cit., paras 3.2–3.4.
90. Op. cit., Parts 2 and 3.
91. Op. cit., Appendix B.
92. See, for example, (1999) 20 *The Company Lawyer*, special edition (June 1999).
93. Op. cit., Chapter 2. See, for example, the Strategic Framework, op. cit., paras 2.4–2.7 and its use of the terms 'efficient' and 'efficiency'. *Developing the Framework,* op. cit., is perhaps sharper in its focus concluding that the objective in the area of corporate governance should be to 'ensure optimal conditions for efficient operation of companies … in a way which … minimises … so called "agency costs" …', para. 2.5.
94. Cheffins, B. R., *Company Law* (Oxford: Clarendon).
95. Dias, R. W. M., 'The Value of a Value Study of Law', (1965) *Modern Law Review* 397; and Dias, *Jurisprudence* (Butterworths, 1985), Chapter 10.
96. Op. cit., paras 1.9–1.10.
97. Op. cit., para. 1.2.
98. Op. cit., Part 3.
99. Op. cit., Part 2.
100. Op. cit. paras 4.4. and 4.5.
101. Paras 2.10–2.19.
102. Involving mobility of business and capital, globalisation of brands and the ability of firms to operate internationally without local incorporation.
103. Involving both globalisation and the participation of the UK in the EC legal harmonisation programme. The role of the European Convention on Human Rights is considered in para. 3.8.
104. Company law was seen as only one of a number of sources of regulatory control of companies, alongside the Stock Exchange and other bodies.
105. Company law was seen as depending on information, and information technology was therefore seen as capable of transforming the processes and the substantive relationships involved.
106. Reflecting that the largest institutional investors are now consistently large companies' largest shareholders while the overwhelming majority of companies are small owner-managed businesses.
107. Reflecting that the pattern of productive activity for many sectors of the economy was shifting to become increasingly human resource and knowledge-based and asset structures were changing with company assets increasingly 'soft' for example brands.
108. Reflecting the major role these play in the economy and the failure of company law to pay attention to their peculiar needs.
109. Op. cit., p. 11.
110. Op. cit., p. 15.
111. Op. cit., para. 3.25.
112. See Cadbury Committee Report, op. cit., para. 1.1, Greenbury Study Group Report, op. cit., para. 1.10 and Hampel Committee Report, op. cit., paras 1.1 and 1.16.
113. Op. cit., para. 1.9.
114. Op. cit., paras 1.6–1.8.
115. Op. cit., 1.21 and 1.18.
116. Op. cit., para. 2.8.
117. Op. cit., p. i.
118. Op. cit., paras 2.4 and 2.6.
119. Op. cit., para. 2.4.
120. Op. cit., para. 1.7.
121. Op. cit., para. 1.4.
122. Op. cit., para. 14.10.
123. Op. cit., para. 3.4.
124. Op. cit., para. 5.1.32.
125. Op. cit., paras 3.137–3.141.
126. Op. cit., para. 2.7.
127. Op. cit., para. 1.6.
128. Op. cit., para. 1.16.
129. Op. cit., p. 26.
130. Op. cit., para. 3.7.
131. Op. cit., para. 3.7.
132. Op. cit., paras 5.1.12–5.1.13.
133. Op. cit., para. 5.1.8.
134. Op. cit., para. 5.1.15.

135. Op. cit., Chapter 2. The changes actually proposed are summarised in paras 2.19–2.26.
136. Op. cit., para. 3.21.
137. Op. cit., paras 3.24–3.25.
138. Op. cit., paras 3.26 –3.31.
139. It is interesting to observe the case studies set out by Higginson, R., op. cit, Chapter 1, of the experiences of Christians in business and of churches' approaches to business.
140. See forthcoming Cambridge Paper by Schulter, M., 'Risk, Reward and Responsibility: Limited Liability and Company Reform', where this argument is powerfully advanced.
141. See Garnett, J., *Evangelicalism and Business in Evangelical Faith and Public Zeal*, ed. Wolffe, J. (SPCK, 1995), Chapter 3, especially pp. 69–70.
142. See, for example, the *Company Directors Disqualification Act 1986* and s. 214 *Insolvency Act 1986*.
143. See further Copp, S. F., 'A Christian Vision for Corporate Governance', op. cit.
144. See Freeman, R. E., *Strategic Planning: A Stakeholder Approach* (Pitman Publishing, 1984), p. 31, cited by Sternberg, E., 'The Defects of Stakeholder Theory' (1997), 5 *Corporate Governance* 3.
145. Moore, G., 'Tinged shareholder theory: or what's so special about stakeholders?' (1999), 8 *Business Ethics: A European Review* 117.
146. Op. cit., paras 3.2–3.4.
147. Op. cit., para. 1.2.
148. Op. cit., p. 25.
149. Op. cit., paras 5.1.10, 5.1.12 and 5.1.39.
150. Although it must be borne in mind that a wide variety of conduct is in fact regulated by other areas of company law such as the *Company Directors' Disqualification Act 1986,* and, for example, the general criminal law.
151. Memorandum 255, *The Reform of Company Law.*
152. Op. cit., pp. 25–6.
153. Op. cit., paras 3.2–3.4.
154. Op. cit., pp. 16–17.

5
Medical Dilemmas and the Law

Alastair V. Campbell
PROFESSOR OF ETHICS IN MEDICINE, UNIVERSITY OF BRISTOL

Ann Nelson (chair) and Prof. Alastair V. Campbell

INTRODUCTION

Nearly fifty years ago Rene Dubos concluded his remarkable book *Mirage of Health,*[1] with these prophetic words:

> The earth is not a resting place ... To grow in the midst of dangers is the
> fate of the human race, because it is the law of the spirit.

This insight into the restless, questing character of human nature seems nowhere more evident than in the transformations of medicine in the last decades of the twentieth century. Long gone are the days when a minister, following the instructions of the *First Book of Discipline,* will make every visit to the sick an occasion to advise the patient to prepare to meet his Maker, by confessing his sins and reconciling himself with his neighbours. Far more likely is a discussion of the hopes of cure which medicine seems to promise every sufferer, a new drug, a new surgical technique, even a new body part. At the turn of the twenty-first century, with the dramatic advances in human genetics arising from the Human Genome Project, we seem to have stumbled on the secret of life itself, to have cracked the Creator's own code, giving us unimagined powers of repairing or changing our own physical nature.

So we no longer regard the doctor as merely delaying the inevitable, a caring companion on our mortal journey, who can be relied upon always to comfort, to relieve our pain often, but rarely to cure. Now – with the encouragement of governments who want more 'responsible' patients – we see ourselves as consumers of a product, which should fulfil our needs and meet our aspirations. This might be regarded as some kind of growing up – a move from the childishly trusting compliant patient, to the informed and articulate adult consumer – but it is far from the 'growth in the midst of dangers' described by Dubos. We recall the title of his book – *Mirage of Health.* There is no genuine growth in a demand for perfection, a denial of our finitude, a wish for total control, or a refusal to see our essential dependency as humans. These are part of the illusion, of the *mirage* of health. True growth, genuine health, comes in the struggle with adversity, not in the pretence that we need never face it.

It is against this background that I wish to consider how the law, Christian ethics and current dilemmas in medicine interrelate. My thesis is that some of the changes now being sought in the law are reflections in this dramatic shift in attitudes towards medicine and the medical profession, and so they must be regarded with great caution and subjected to a critical appraisal by Christian ethics. My argument could easily be misunderstood. I am not deploring the amazing achievements of modern medicine in combating or preventing deadly diseases and in increasing life expectancy by improving the health of the population. Nor am I a defender of those who want to continue an arrogant medical paternalism that treats the patient as a helpless child, to be given the minimum of information and exhorted to obey doctor's orders. Medicine has brought great benefit to humankind. And the move towards greater autonomy of patients and respect for their own decision-making capacity is a clear moral gain, reflecting Kant's categorical imperative, to treat all persons as ends in themselves, never as mere means. Moreover, it is demonstrably the case that, when people regain a sense of control of their own lives, despite illness or disability, their health and sense of wellbeing improve. However, the Kantian emphasis on the autonomy of the rational moral agent is only part of a fully adequate account of human nature, so far as Christian ethics is concerned. All human endeavours, including science and medicine, become idolatrous when they seek to take the place of God, by making claims (or having illusions projected on to them) with respect to human fulfilment or spiritual wholeness. Science, medicine and their associated technologies, *are* mere means, and such means can bring weal or woe, the fulfilment of human nature or the frustration of that potential for fulfilment, which is the gift of our Creator.

Modern medicine is replete with moral dilemmas arising from the extraordinary expansion of our choices. But in this lecture I shall select just two areas of potential legislative change: moves to legalise voluntary euthanasia (or physician-assisted suicide); and legislative changes which may be required to meet new opportunities for genetic manipulation of human cells. Each of these areas raises issues of major concern for Christian ethics. Of course, in a democratic and pluralist society, laws will be enacted which contravene Christian values, but that should not prevent us providing a well-reasoned critique, which can appeal to a wider community than those with Christian belief. In any case, critique need not mean opposition to eventual legislation. It merely seeks to ensure the whole range of human values is considered, not only those fashionable in our age. This is especially important in my second topic area, the possibilities emerging from new discoveries in human genetics. The questions raised here are so novel, that there can be no obvious or stock answers, from Christian tradition or any other source. What is needed is as rich an account as possible of the values entailed.

THE END OF LIFE – SHOULD EUTHANASIA BE LEGALISED?

There is a continuing debate in the UK about whether the law should be changed to allow doctors to take active steps to end a patient's life or to assist them to commit suicide. Both are clearly criminal acts at present. So far as active euthanasia is concerned, the law makes no distinction between 'mercy killing' of an incurably or terminally ill patient and murder. The legal position is captured by Lord Devlin:

> If the acts done are intended to kill and do, in fact, kill, it does not matter if a life is cut short by weeks or months, it is just as much murder as if it were cut short by years.[2]

In the case of 'physician-assisted suicide', a doctor counselling or assisting suicide would be guilty of an offence under the Suicide Act 1961, as would any other person. That Act abolished the offences of suicide or attempted suicide, but retained assisting suicide as a crime, presumably in order to defend vulnerable parties from undue influence.

It is important to distinguish these actions from what is sometimes called 'passive euthanasia', by which is meant the withdrawing or withholding of potentially life-saving measures. The law gives a legally competent person the unqualified right to refuse any treatment, whether or not that refusal will lead to the person's death. In addition a doctor is entitled to withdraw or withhold potentially life-prolonging treatment, if it can be shown that it will not be effective in either maintaining or restoring the health of the patient.[3] A doctor may also prescribe drugs required to relieve a patient's pain or respiratory distress, even though another effect of those drugs may be to shorten the patient's life. However, the dosage must be commensurate with the purpose of relieving the distress only. An excessive dose will be seen as fulfilling an intention to kill the patient, not merely to alleviate distress, and so will be a criminal act.

A number of recent events have provoked continuing debate about whether the law at present is adequate or fair. In 1992 Dr Cox, a rheumatologist who injected an incurable patient in persistent unrelieved pain with a poisonous substance (potassium chloride), was found guilty of attempted murder. However, the judge did not administer an immediate custodial sentence and the General Medical Council merely admonished him and required him to undergo further training. It was clear that public and professional sentiment had much sympathy for Dr Cox and had difficulty with a law which classed him as a murderer. (The case contrasts sharply with the more recent conviction of Dr Shipman, the medical serial killer.) Moreover, although the legal prohibition of euthanasia is virtually universal, an exception is found in the Netherlands, where euthanasia, if requested by the patient, can be carried out, provided certain conditions are fulfilled; and in the USA the State of Oregon has legalised a form of physician-assisted suicide (PAS) in a 'Death with Dignity' Act. These changes have led the BMA, at the request of its membership, to revisit its opposition to euthanasia and PAS, and an extensive consensus conference on the latter was held in March 2000. (Nevertheless the BMA's position remains the same, with a majority regarding a change in the law as undesirable.)

There is also considerable unease regarding the validity of the active/ passive distinction which forbids killing but allows discontinuation of life-saving measures. It has been long criticised by philosophers (eg Jonathan Glover, Michael Tooley[4]) on the grounds that if the death of the patient is a foreseen consequence then there can be no moral difference between killing and omitting life-saving measures. Advocates of voluntary euthanasia use this philosophical criticism to argue that the law is incoherent, and that if a competent person can legally refuse treatment they should also have a legal right to request the means to end their own lives. Moreover, some *opponents* of euthanasia are equally uneasy with the current legal authorisation of treatment withdrawal decisions. The 1993 Bland case, in which the withdrawal of artificial means of providing nutrition and hydration from a patient in Persistent Vegetative State was permitted, made both advocates for, and opponents of, euthanasia claim that the acts/omissions doctrine was unsustainable.

Christian ethics and voluntary euthanasia

Is it then time to change the law? Should Christians, out of compassion for those who suffer from irremediable conditions or unremitting pain and out of respect for the motives of those doctors who want to help their patients to gain a swift and peaceful death, support the campaign for voluntary euthanasia? The classic Christian theological answer to this is that Christians must respect the sanctity of all human life, including their own. Life is a gift of God, not a human possession to be disposed of at will. This euthanasia and suicide are denials of the sovereignty of God and cannot be viewed by Christians as morally acceptable.[5]

However, this account of Christian obligation may be questioned. Robin Gill has cogently revealed the ambiguity of the concept of life as a divine gift:

> Gift relationships are by no means all gracious – some can be highly manipulative, especially the required gifts of submission. Gracious gifts should be treated with gratitude and responsibility, but they should not bind the one to whom they are given – it is manipulative gifts that do that … Gracious gifts leave both giver and receiver free. Indeed when God-given life becomes nothing but a burden, it might seem appropriate to return that life prayerfully and humbly to the giver.[6]

Similar considerations lead Paul Badham to argue that support of voluntary euthanasia reflects Christian values, notably compassion for the sick, a respect for the primacy of free choice and the opportunity for a prayerful death. Badham portrays the death experienced in modern medical facilities as 'a lonely and degrading extension of the dying process', and paints a rosy picture of an arranged death with family present and the minister offering words of prayer and consolation to all.[7]

The arguments for and against euthanasia are complex, and I cannot do full justice to them all here, but it is important to recognise (as Gill certainly does) that we cannot isolate the question of legalising medical killing on request or medical assistance in suicide from the effects of such change in the law on our social values, attitudes and expectations. (Gill describes the 'procedural slippage' which has occurred in the practice of abortion, since the UK Abortion Act, and fears a similar slide of euthanasia is legalised. He foresees the emergence of a less compassionate society, in which the vulnerable are pressured into considering 'voluntary' euthanasia.) I share these concerns, but more fundamentally I am concerned about the changes in our understanding of medicine and in our concept of care for the sick which such a change in the law would symbolise. As a conclusion to this section let me describe this concern and relate it to the general approach outlined in my Introduction.

We need to ask what is the primary purpose of laws, which relate to homicide and to abetting suicide? I suggest that they are connected to the most basic value enshrined in Christian ethics, which is God's concern for the weakest and most vulnerable in our society. The law should not promote the freedom of the strong so much as defend the weak from those who hold power, whether that be the power of wealth, political influence, or of sheer physical force. Medicine aligns itself with this fundamental value. It is a reaching out, without partiality or prejudice, to those who are most in need.

What then would it mean to encompass in law the right to request one's own demise by medical means? I see it as yet another extension of the claim of the articulate and influential members of society to have all their wishes met, not as a defence of the weak and the vulnerable. Those most at risk would be the conscientious elderly, who, now seeing themselves as a burden on family and society, would be given encouragement by the law itself to make a swift and decent exit. For this reason, Christian ethics should oppose moves to legalise voluntary euthanasia because, in its assertion of a 'right to death', it is advancing yet further the interests of one group rather than seeing the place of law in defence of the community as a whole. It is true that the law as it stands restricts individual autonomy in the sphere of arranging one's own death, but there is nothing unusual in such restrictions, when they are necessary to protect the interests of all. In the service of a truly caring community we need to retain laws that prevent the deliberate taking of another life, even at that person's request.

Defenders of legalising euthanasia may see this approach as lacking in compassion, but that is only so if it is genuinely true that we cannot manage death in a way that preserves dignity, controls pain and provides companionship. The hospice movement has demonstrated that such things are indeed entirely possible. It is only a matter of political will to provide adequate facilities and training to enable the excellence of hospice care to be a feature of all NHS terminal care. Priorities in social policy should be directed to that end, and the law should not enshrine the administering of lethal measures as part of the medical or any other profession's duty to care.

THE BEGINNING OF LIFE – WHAT ARE THE LIMITS TO OUR CREATIVE POSSIBILITIES?

I turn from the control of death to the control of life itself. It would be impossible to exaggerate the significance of recent developments in genetics, which have unlocked many of the secrets of how living organisms, including humans, develop from the single cell to the fully grown adult. The worldwide publicity surrounding the cloning of Dolly here in Edinburgh is merely one indication of the significance of this area not only for reproductive medicine, but also for the development of revolutionary new therapies. In particular, so-called 'therapeutic cloning', the production of compatible tissues or organs by creating stem cells which would be genetically virtually identical to the adult requiring the therapy, seems to offer new hope to sufferers from a wide range of conditions.

Another potential for therapy emerging from the cell nuclear replacement technique pioneered with Dolly is the avoidance of diseases associated with the mitochondria – the surrounding matter of the ovum – by placing the nucleus of the mother's ovum in an enucleated donor ovum. Using this 'repaired egg' one could proceed to fertilisation with the partner's sperm, leading to a child without mitochondrial defects. It should be stressed that all these possible therapeutic developments are at a very early stage and that much basic research using human cells would be needed before the therapeutic applications could even be attempted.

Table 5.1
Possible uses of tissue derived from stem cells to treat disease

Cell type	Target disease
Neural (nerve) cells	Stroke, Parkinson's disease, spinal cord injury, multiple sclerosis
Heart muscle cells	Heart attacks, congestive heart failure
Insulin-producing cells	Diabetes
Cartilage cells	Osteoarthritis
Blood cells	Cancer, immunodeficiencies, inherited blood diseases, leukaemia
Liver cells	Hepatitis, cirrhosis
Skin cells	Burns, wound healing
Bone cells	Osteoporosis
Retinal (eye) cells	Macular degeneration
Skeletal muscle cells	Muscular dystrophy

Much helpful Christian commentary has already been offered in this area – not least by the Church of Scotland's Science, Religion and Technology Unit. I do not intend to go into the detail of that commentary in this lecture but will simply highlight what I see as the main issue of concern, as we consider legislative possibilities. The issue is summarised in my subheading – what are the limits to our creative possibilities? This could be seen as either a question of fact or a question of value. If it is a factual question, then events over the past decade suggest that the possibilities are virtually limitless. Already we can predict a whole range of genetic conditions and avoid them by selective implantation of embryos or by selective termination of pregnancy. But equally these techniques allow for selection of the preferred gender, even though most countries seek to outlaw this application. As the Human Genome Project comes to an end, we can expect much more detailed knowledge of our genetic inheritance giving the basis for genetic manipulation to produce desired characteristics and avoid undesired ones. Despite worldwide opposition to human reproductive cloning and to germline modification of humans, we can safely predict that both will be attempted soon in some country without clear laws preventing such work.

But what if we pose the question about limits to our creativity in a normative rather than a descriptive fashion? What limits *should* we impose? Some would say that this is a pointless question, since science will not be prevented from proceeding, however much we might seek to control it. This seems to me a counsel of despair, which would stop us putting legislative controls on any human activity, however detrimental, on the grounds that it will happen anyway. I would suggest that we are in a unique position to consider the normative issues, as the science is still at a very early stage. This is especially so in the UK, in view of our experience with an early piece of legislation in the field – the Human Fertilisation and Embryology Act (HFE Act) of 1990. We cannot control the world scientific community, but we should be guiding our own scientists by discussing how their discoveries may meet genuinely human ends, and by creating laws that enable this to happen.

How then might the law and Christian ethics interrelate in this difficult area of limits to our creativity? Let us recall the current provisions of the HFE Act. Following extensive debate in the Warnock Commission and in Parliament, the Act, which was passed in 1990, provides a legislative framework for the provision of assisted reproductive interventions, including donor insemination and in vitro fertilisation. Through a system of licensing it seeks to ensure that clinics provide services in ways to safeguard the welfare of children born by these means. The Act also permits research on human embryos up to a limit of fourteen days' development, and these embryos may be 'spare' ones donated by the couple seeking treatment or they may be created specifically for the purposes of the research.[8] Research on human embryos can be carried out only for specific purposes, which are related to infertility treatment, contraception, miscarriage, detection of genetic abnormalities or understanding the causes of genetic disease. However, additional purposes may be added by affirmative regulations, which would have to be tabled in Parliament.

It should be noted that the UK is relatively unusual in Europe, since it permits the creation of human embryos for research. This is prohibited by the 1997 European Convention on Human Rights and Biomedicine.[9] (The UK has not yet signed the Convention and if it did so it could claim exemption from this provision.) This permission in the Act, together with the power to add other purposes, means that research into cloned human stem cells and research into nuclear replacement as a treatment for mitochondrial disease[10] could be made legal in the UK.

What then, from the perspective of Christian ethics, should be done in the sphere of legislative change (if any)? What limits *should* there be on this remarkable potential for human creativity? It has to be said that this is a difficult area for many Christians. The HFE Act, like the Abortion Act, removes protection from the human embryo, permitting its use as means to an end and, in most cases of research, its destruction. For those who regard the embryo as a person with the same rights as a living child, the existing legislation is immoral, and any extension of the purposes of the HFE Act can only make matters worse, by allowing more research in which embryos will be destroyed. Some Christians may see the use of 'spare' embryos from fertility treatment as justifiable, since they would in any event be destroyed eventually, but would oppose the creation of embryos solely for the purposes of research.[11] However, limiting research to spare embryos would prevent any work on producing cells for creating compatible tissue, since this must entail the creation of an embryo using the nucleus of a cell from the affected adult. It follows that the most important line of therapeutic development depends (at least in its initial stages) on treating a human embryo solely as a source of material for the benefit of others. If the research is successful – and that cannot be known for some years – we are using our new knowledge of the genesis of human life to produce, not a new individual life, but replicas of a living person's tissue. We would be producing at will the constituent materials of a living human organism.

How are we to assess this theologically? (I leave aside now the objection to all of this on the grounds that the embryo is a person, since such a view makes it clear that research now taking place is wrong, never mind these developments.) I suppose what is startling is that we have tended to see the creation of life itself as somehow the prerogative of God alone, a reserved area, as it were, into which humans cannot or should not enter. Yet from the earliest emergence of human culture we have been co-creators with God. That has been our blessing and our curse. We have been able to take all that stuff around us, including our own bodies and brains, and re-order it in a myriad of ways. What is there that can be exempt from the touch of the human hand and the ingenuity of the human mind and imagination? In our amazing era we have discovered that life itself is open to our manipulation. It seems undeniable that our Creator has made us so that even that door is open to us. We are co-creators of organic life itself and can shape it virtually as we will.

I would argue, perhaps surprisingly, that the first task of Christian ethics is to *celebrate* this enlarging of our powers, not to deplore or fear it. Some would see this as blasphemy, human arrogance as old as Eden, thinking the serpent's lie, that we shall be 'as gods'. But the truth is that we *have* been given the power, we *are* co-creators. The danger is not blasphemy, but idolatry. For, the second task of Christian ethics is to warn us against a worship of that power for its own sake or to use it to create idols of our own making. What images might we create with this power of life itself? Will we deny our mortality and pour countless millions into high-cost therapy at the end of life, manufacturing ever more replacements for our ageing body parts? Will we worship intellect and try to create a society where only the intelligent are valued? Will we worship height, or physical strength or physical appearance, and use our power to make false images of human worth culled from our own prejudices and preferences? Or might we use our power to help some of the terrible distress that our fellow humans suffer – burn victims in need of skin that will restore their damaged bodies; people with chronic disease of mind or body, like multiple sclerosis, Parkinson's disease, Alzheimer's disease, osteoarthritis, leukaemia, whose damaged or affected tissue might be replaced; children battling against the horrors of muscular dystrophy?

There is at the centre of Christian ethics the figure of Christ, revealing what God wants of us in our co-creation. That figure, as the Bible attests, is utterly removed from the idolatry of our cultural icons of material or sporting success, physical allure and social advantage. The crucified Christ signifies weakness, despair and defeat, an ugly sight from which people avert their eyes: yet here above all is compassion and hope for the disfigured in mind and body; a love that risks all to make people whole.

I conclude that, despite the real offence that the use of embryos as research material must cause many Christians, there is a case, based on Christian ethics, for supporting a legislative change, broadening the purpose of the HFE Act. I say this with considerable caution, for, it is clear that developments in genetics and cell therapy could take us down a path of prejudice, social discrimination and futile high-cost medicine, as I have described above. But I see the task to be to *shape* legislation and licensing controls that will ensure the humanitarian potential of these rapid changes in the technology of biomedicine, not to oppose *all legislative* change. I remain, however, conscious of the risks in this way of proceeding. We are co-creators with God, because that is the divine will for us, but we are also creatures of sin, lacking the wisdom and the love of our own

Creator. We must, therefore, surely experience the same trepidation that the poet, R. S. Thomas, describes in the heart of God, as he wrestles – as though at Peniel – with the hand he has created:

The Hand

It was a hand.

God looked at it and looked away.

There was a coldness about his heart,

as though the hand clasped it.

At the end of a dark tunnel,

he saw cities the hand would build,

engines that it would raze them with …

Tempted to undo the joints of the fingers,

he picked it up.

But the hand wrestled with him.

'Tell me your name' it cried,

'and I will write it in bright hold …'

But God, feeling the nails in his side …

fought on in silence.

This was the long war with himself always foreseen,

the question not to be answered.

What is the hand for? …

'I let you go', he said,

'but without blessing'.

Notes

1. *Mirage of Health: Utopias, Progress and Biological Change* (New York: Harper, 1959), p. 235.
2. Devlin, J., quoted in Mason, J. K. and McCall Smith, R. A., *Law and Medical Ethics*, 4th edition (Edinburgh: Butterworths, 1994), p. 317.
3. See BMA, *Withholding and Withdrawing Treatment* (London: BMA publications, 1999).
4. J. Glover, *Causing Deaths and Saving Lives* (London: Penguin Books, 1977); M. Tooley, *Abortion and Infanticide* (Oxford: Clarendon Press, 1983).
5. Pope John Paul II, *Evangelium Vitae* (published as *The Gospel of Life*, New York: Random House, 1995), paras 12 and 28.
6. Gill, R. (ed.), *Euthanasia and the Churches* (London: Cassell, 1998), p. 25f.
7. Ibid., p. 58.
8. In practice very few embryos have been created. The figures are 48,000 donated and 118 created from 1992 to 1998.
9. Article 18.2.
10. Muscle, heart, brain and eye are all affected by mitochondrial defects. There are more than fifty inherited diseases of metabolism known to be caused by defects in mitochondrial DNA.
11. This was the position of the late Tony Dyson, when he served on the Warnock Commission, and it has been endorsed recently by the US National Bioethics Advisory Commission.

6
Christianity and Law Reform: A Living Tradition

Paul Beaumont
PROFESSOR OF EUROPEAN UNION AND PRIVATE INTERNATIONAL LAW,
UNIVERSITY OF ABERDEEN

Prof. Paul Beaumont and Rev. Prof. Duncan B. Forrester (chair)

A CLEAR CHRISTIAN WORLD-VIEW DOES NOT LEAD TO A CLEAR VIEW OF WHAT MODERN LAW SHOULD BE

At least among Christians who hold to an orthodox position there is a shared belief that people need to have the opportunity to come to know Jesus Christ as the person who can bring meaning and purpose to life: indeed who can enable men and women to enter into a right relationship with God the Father, experience the presence of God's Holy Spirit in their lives, and enjoy eternal life with God. Christians have a strong commitment to be guided by God as to how to live their lives and see the Bible as the key guide to knowing what God intends for his followers. So Christians will agree, at least, on the need to argue for laws that give people freedom to choose to follow Jesus Christ and to live lives according to the teaching laid down in the Bible. This is true even though they disagree among themselves as to the detail of how the biblical teaching should be applied today and the extent to which Christian standards should be incorporated into laws that apply to all people in society.

In a paper given at the Law and Religion Colloquium on 4 July 2000 at University College, London,[1] I set out and examined three propositions about what is the core of Christian Perspectives on the Law:

a) Christianity does tolerate a wide range of views on what the law in a given modern society should be because Jesus did not prescribe a set of laws by which society should be governed but rather sought to bring about changed lives in his followers who would live up to higher standards than external laws can impose and be salt and light in the wider community. (Matthew 5:13–16)

b) Christians should be free to live their lives in accordance with Christ's teaching and therefore it is legitimate to argue for such freedom in a democratic society.

c) Christians are called by Christ to be salt and light in the wider community and therefore it is reasonable for Christians to advocate the benefits of the Christian life for society as a whole. Much of this will be done by seeking to persuade individuals to become Christians but there can also be a role for seeking to influence the lawmaking process. Here Christians will be cautious because they are aware that the Bible does not provide a template for modern law and because they are passionate advocates of giving people freedom of conscience. Nonetheless there may be norms which can be agreed with and adhered to by people who are not Christians which Christians may wish to advocate.

So it is possible to categorise a modern agenda for Christian law reformers as falling into the defensive category of (b) above of protecting the ability of Christians to live their lives in accordance with Christian principles and the more outward-looking approach of seeking to influence the law as it applies to the whole of society in (c) above. The problem is that the categorisation is not watertight. Take for example the plans of Lord Mackay of Clashfern to change the divorce laws in England and Wales. One of the problems of moving from a fault to a no-fault system is that it leaves the Christian spouse who is opposed to divorce able to be divorced by the other spouse (who is also a Christian) even though a strict biblical reading would give no ground for such a divorce.[2] Lord Mackay was motivated by Christian principles to try and improve the lot of divorcing people and their children[3] and was concerned with (c) above. He was particularly anxious to take account of the 'realities of the human condition' and the need for Christians to demonstrate God's 'grace' in their law reform proposals, but fully supported the idea that 'the process of law reform in a modern secular democracy be informed by biblical perspectives'.[4] However, when the secular law becomes divorced from the high standards to be applied by Christians it has the knock-on consequence of making it difficult for a Christian to live in accordance with Christian teachings on divorce unless his or her Christian spouse continues to hold to those teachings. This illustrates the difficulty of even achieving the defensive objective in (b) because society has to take account not only of the way in which non-Christians want to live but also Christians who find it difficult to comply with Christ's teachings (which to an extent we all do).

Before turning to some examples of areas where Christians have had or are seeking to have a bearing on law reform it may be helpful to point out that there are Christian agencies trying to influence law reform like the Evangelical Alliance, CARE and the Christian Institute. This is in addition to the work of the Christian denominations and churches. I am involved in the Lawyers' Christian Fellowship (LCF). It is an organisation of some 1300 to 1500 lawyers in the UK which has been in existence for nearly 150 years. It has traditionally focused on fellowship among Christian lawyers, prayer and evangelism. These are still priorities but in recent years it has sought to influence reform of the law. The organisation has grown from having no full-time staff just six years or so ago to having two full-timers and four part-timers now. The attention to law reform is seen in a few ways:

1. Specialist groupings within LCF prepare responses on developments within their area, eg on family law.

2. The London group has organised a series of keynote talks on topical law reform issues over the last two years.

3. The new Director of LCF, Christine John, is committed to giving LCF a

stronger voice in law reform and is setting up law reform groups in England and Wales and in Scotland.

4. Student LCF groups around the UK are grappling with how to apply their faith to the legal issues they are studying.

5. The LCF in Scotland has had a devolved structure for a number of years with a Scottish Committee led by the Scottish Chairman, currently David Laing, and this year the Scottish Conference examined law reform issues.

6. Since 1996 LCF Academics have met in annual conference to address a wide variety of legal issues from the perspective of a Christian world-view. This has led to a series of books on Christian Perspectives on the Law published by Paternoster Press.[5]

It is the last development with which I have been most closely involved and will draw on extensively in considering some of the key areas where it is arguable that a tradition of Christian law reform is emerging.

FAMILY LAW REFORM IN ENGLAND AND WALES UNDER A CHRISTIAN LORD CHANCELLOR

Lord Mackay of Clashfern is the President of the Lawyers' Christian Fellowship and a committed Christian. As Lord Chancellor he was responsible for the Bill which became the Family Law Act 1996 and was intended to reform the law of divorce in England and Wales.[6] Lord Mackay was fully aware of the New Testament teaching on divorce and summed it up as follows:

Divorce on the ground of adultery by one party or such desertion by one party as could not be healed by the church or the civil magistrate is I think a reasonable account of the passages in the New Testament which deal with this subject.[7]

This is clearly a fault-based system. Many Christians, including Baroness Young, CARE and a minority of the Lawyers' Christian Fellowship, urged Lord

Mackay to adopt a fault-based system in his reform of divorce law. These Christians felt that the previous reform of the divorce law in England and Wales had made a mistake in departing from a fault-based system and introducing what purported to be a no-fault system with one ground for divorce – the irretrievable breakdown of the marriage.[8] In fact the legislation provided only five facts upon which the irretrievable breakdown of the marriage could be proven. Three of the five 'facts' were fault-based (adultery, desertion and 'unreasonable behaviour' – a watering down of the previous cruelty)[8] and two were genuinely no fault (two years separation and mutual consent and five years separation with no consent). These Christians felt that one of the reasons for the rising divorce rate was that the 1969 reforms had made it easier to get divorced and in some respects departed from the fault principle which is at the basis of the New Testament teaching on divorce. Society should show its commitment to marriage by making divorce more difficult not easier.

Instead Lord Mackay advocated a completely no-fault system for the granting of a divorce.[9] The key feature of the reform was that divorce would become automatic a certain period of time after it was first sought by one of the spouses.[10] The correct time period was a matter for debate but the departure from a fault-based system was essential to the idea. How could such a unilateral approach to divorce be proposed by a Christian?

First, Lord Mackay was unhappy about how the fault-based system was working. People who wanted a divorce quickly were deliberately committing adultery to achieve that objective and thereby becoming free to remarry. Lord Mackay commented that:

> This was giving an effect to fault, particularly adultery, which in my judgement sent a very strange message to the public.[12]

Perhaps Lord Mackay was concerned that the fault-based system was actually encouraging people to sin by making adultery the quickest and simplest way to get divorced. He was also of the view from his own experience of the courts that insistence on proof of fault 'made no contribution to preventing marital breakdown'.[13] Furthermore, he felt that the fault-based system further damaged the already damaged relationship between the parties because of the requirement to make allegations which might be exaggerated. In turn these allegations could be very damaging on the children. Lord Mackay is conscious of the argument that he retained fault as a factor in splitting property and in terms of who should have custody of the children and is therefore wide open to the allegation that this will damage the relationship between the parties and harm the children anyway. Lord Mackay's response is that this might be a justifiable price to pay when trying to make the correct decision about property rights and the care of the children but not 'where the only practical result was to give an earlier divorce'.[14] Another defect of the old law was that the parties could get divorced without sorting out the arrangements for the children or how the property was to be split. This had the danger that people could get divorced without counting the true cost in human or emotional terms. If people were required to resolve these issues before divorce they might think better of the divorce or at least minimise the harm to the children by agreeing suitable arrangements for their upbringing and making sure that the financial resources were divided appropriately.

So Lord Mackay was convinced that a fault-based system did not save marriages, that in practice it was probably encouraging the sin of adultery, widening the rift between the parties and harming the children. With respect, his other points about not resolving the financial arrangements and the care of the children before the divorce have got nothing to do with a fault or no-fault system. He could have retained a fault-based system but reformed the divorce procedure so that a divorce could not be granted until these issues were resolved by consent between the parties or, if necessary, by the court. It was on the basis of another procedural reform that Lord Mackay hoped he could save some marriages. The 1996 Act would make it compulsory for the person seeking the divorce to have an information meeting[15] at the beginning of the divorce process during which the true cost of the divorce in terms of the likely financial arrangements and custody arrangements would be pointed out. Lord Mackay wanted this meeting to be a 'facility for persuading the parties not to proceed to divorce' and to act as a 'disincentive to going ahead with divorce'.[16] I think the information meeting is an admirable idea but this reform could have been made while retaining fault-based grounds of divorce. To be fair it might have had less chance of succeeding in persuading the parties not to divorce if during the meeting there had to be an explanation that to get divorced the spouses did not just need to wait for a certain period of time but rather had to prove fault. The mention of fault might induce the parties to think of the bad things the other party had done rather than seek a reconciliation.

Apart from the information meeting the other key feature of the Mackay proposals was that there should be a reasonably substantial period of time before a divorce could be granted. He rejected any exception to this:

> because once an exception was made I felt the whole rule was likely ultimately to be disregarded. An exception would also be likely to erode the idea of commitment that I felt should be involved in marriage.[17]

Of course Lord Mackay was resisting a fault-based exception which would allow divorce quicker than the normal period. However, would not a truly Christian divorce law have combined the information meeting, the cooling-off period of at least a year, a requirement to resolve the financial and custody issues before the divorce is granted, and the need to prove adultery or desertion. This might indeed be an ideal divorce law for a Christian community and the standard that Christians should aspire to no matter what the law of the land is.

However, Lord Mackay was conscious that he was legislating for the whole community of England and Wales, not just the Christians within it. His justification for making the civil law, in relation to the grounds of divorce, more liberal than those permitted by Christ for Christians is based on a close exegesis of Matthew 19. He said:

> But the real question for me was should the civil law permit divorce in any circumstances other than those which I have mentioned [adultery and desertion] as regarded as grounds for divorce under the New Testament arrangements. It was significant to me that the Lord Jesus in answering question on the subject told his inquisitors that Moses had allowed divorce because of the hardness of their hearts but that from the beginning it was not so. He also indicated that someone who divorced his wife other than on the ground of adultery caused her to commit adultery and this, I took it, implied that the civil arrangements might make this possible. If the civil arrangements did not it was difficult to see how our Lord's judgment on the conduct of someone

who put away his wife other than on the ground of adultery could be realistic.[18]

The problem with Lord Mackay's analysis of Matthew 19 is that Jesus at no time suggests that the civil law should be more liberal than the Christian standard. He impliedly accepts that it is more liberal but neither condemns nor condones this fact. If Lord Mackay is relying on Jesus' silence in not condemning liberal standards in the civil law it may be a rather shaky foundation. After all Jesus' statement in Matthew 19:9, 'I tell you that anyone who divorces his wife, except for marital unfaithfulness, and marries another woman commits adultery' was not restricted to his Christian hearers but included the Pharisees who asked the question. Of course one might say that Jesus was only addressing the moral question of what constitutes the sin of adultery rather than the question of what the law ought to be. However, it is difficult for some Christians to advocate a law that by making divorce easier will inevitably lead to more remarriages which are inherently sinful.

Nonetheless, Lord Mackay's reliance on Jesus' silence about what the civil law should be may not be so shaky. It may be an early sign of an acceptance of the importance of freedom of conscience for the unbeliever. This was a principle passionately argued for by Roger Williams, the seventeenth-century puritan, and is now a key part of much of Christian thinking.[19] It is hard for a Christian to accept but nonetheless a reality that true freedom of conscience includes freedom to sin. Of course there will be a societal consensus that some sins are so bad that they should be against the law, eg murder, rape and theft, but it may be that there is no consensus that divorce on demand after a time delay (followed by remarriage) should be prohibited by law. In such circumstances some Christians will continue to argue for what they believe to be the best solution, the high biblical standards for divorce, while other Christians will accept that to preserve freedom of conscience for unbelievers this is the type of issue where law and morality can be severed and divorce allowed on more grounds than the Bible indicates or on any grounds. As Christians we can make this choice but we should be very careful to respect those who make a different choice from the one we do. It is valuable that some Christians hold out the high biblical standards on divorce as being the best way for society as part of a process of convincing people that they need to be empowered by the Holy Spirit to live up to such standards. It is also good that some Christians fight for the freedom of non-Christians to reject Jesus' teaching on divorce and to live according to different ethical standards. This is a very important freedom because it is the direct corollary of the freedom of Christians to reject the politically correct norms of today on equality and non-discrimination in choosing to live their lives by high biblical standards.

DEFENCE OF THE IMPORTANCE OF RELIGIOUS FREEDOM WHEN IT CLASHES WITH CONCEPTS OF EQUALITY AND NON-DISCRIMINATION

This is an area where Christians are basically trying to argue for proposition (b) which I mentioned on p. 89. The concern is to have laws which allow Christians and groups of Christians to live in accordance with Christ's teachings.

Fightback by Christian organisations in relation to the Human Rights Bill

The debate surrounding the impact on religious freedom of the Labour Government's desire in the Human Rights Bill to give further effect to the European Convention on Human Rights in the law in the United Kingdom is well documented by Ian Leigh.[20] Churches and Christian organisations were concerned that in some circumstances they would be regarded as 'public authorities'[21] and therefore it would be 'unlawful ... to act in a way which is incompatible with a Convention right'. Even if churches and other Christian organisations are not deemed to be 'public authorities' it is clear that there is an obligation on all persons to give effect to legislation 'in a way which is compatible with the Convention rights'.[22] In the common law area the Convention becomes relevant if a dispute reaches the courts because the court may use the Convention as an aid in developing the common law.[23] Furthermore, the fact that courts and tribunals are 'public authorities' for the purpose of the Human Rights Act[24] means that some judges, including Lord Reed,[25] have argued that the courts must not 'act in a way which is incompatible with a Convention right' and therefore must apply the Convention to disputes between private individuals even where legislative interpretation is not involved. In this matter I prefer the view of Ian Leigh, that the fact that courts and tribunals are public authorities means that the Convention standards are imported only 'into court procedures and discretionary decisions (for example, the scope of remedies awarded)'.[26] Churches were concerned that the prohibition on discrimination in Article 14 of the European Convention on Human Rights might be given more weight by the courts in the UK than the right to freedom of religion in Article 9 of the Convention. This could lead to a situation where church schools or nursing homes, particularly where run by the established Church, would be prevented from hiring only Christian staff. In the passage of the Human Rights Bill in the House of Lords the Christian lobby was successful in persuading their Lordships to pass three amendments to lessen the possible impact of the legislation on religious freedom.[27] However, these amendments were not allowed to stand in the House of Commons and instead the Government agreed to a new provision which became section 13 of the Act:

> If a court's determination of any question arising under this Act might affect the exercise by a religious organisation (itself or its members collectively) of the Convention right to freedom of thought, conscience and religion, it must have particular regard to the importance of that right.

This is an important recognition of the group rights of churches and other religious organisations. It does not give those rights automatic primacy in any clash with other rights, like non-discrimination, but it does give a steer to the courts to give particular weight to the freedom of religion of such bodies in the balancing exercise.[28]

Campaign against the proposal for an EC Directive establishing a general framework for Equal Treatment in Employment and Occupation

The Treaty of Amsterdam introduced a new Article 13 into the EC Treaty which took effect on 1 May 1999. This Article provides that:

> Without prejudice to the other provisions of this Treaty and within the limits of the powers conferred by it upon the Community, the Council, acting unanimously on a proposal from the Commission and after consulting the European Parliament, may take appropriate action to combat discrimination based on sex, racial or ethnic origin, religion or belief, disability, age or sexual orientation.

One of the problems with this elevation of non-discrimination to an area of Community competence is that it is not balanced with any notion that it is appropriate for certain groups to discriminate in order to maintain their identity, eg a political group or a church will discriminate in terms of its membership on the basis of 'belief'. Another problem is that it is not clear how wide the Community competence is because of the ambiguity surrounding the phrase 'within the limits of the powers conferred by it upon the Community'. Employment policy is clearly an area of mixed competence between the Member States and the Community but the division of competence is not clear from the EC Treaty and the general statement about the objectives in this area in Article 136 is said to apply to 'The Community and the Member States'.[29]

The Commission proposal for a Council Directive establishing a general framework for equal treatment in employment and occupation[30] was made on 25 November 1999. It has Article 13 of the EC Treaty as its legal basis and it is expected that the Council will adopt the Directive in the year 2000. The Commission proposal seeks to outlaw direct and indirect discrimination on grounds of 'racial or ethnic origin, religion or belief, disability, age or sexual orientation'.[31] The material scope of the Directive extends beyond employment to self-employment and membership of professional bodies.[32] The Commission proposes that Member States should have the discretion to create two exceptions to the prohibition on discrimination. The first exception would permit discrimination based on one of the discriminatory characteristics (religion, etc) if 'by reason of the nature of the particular occupational activities concerned or of the context in which they are carried out, such a characteristic constitutes a genuine occupational qualification'.[33] This provision, if utilised by the relevant Member State, may make it possible for a firm of Christian lawyers to insist that being a Christian 'constitutes a genuine occupational qualification' because of the Christian 'context' in which they are carried out. The firm would find it harder to argue that a requirement that the person is not a practising homosexual is a genuine occupational qualification unless it could convince the court to give a very broad construction to the 'context' in which the occupational activities are carried out. The argument would be that the firm was made up of only those who are not practising homosexuals and offered legal services on that basis. The second exception proposed by the Commission is that:

Member States may provide that, in the case of public or private organisations which pursue directly and essentially the aim of ideological guidance in the field of religion or belief with respect to education, information and the expression of opinions, and for the particular occupational activities within those organisations which are directly and essentially related to that aim, a difference of treatment based on a relevant characteristic related to religion or belief shall not constitute discrimination where, by reason of the nature of these activities, the characteristic constitutes a genuine occupational qualification.[34]

This exception, if adopted by the relevant Member State, would allow a church to employ only Christians as ministers and Christian schools to employ only Christians as teachers of religious education. However, the church or school might not be allowed to insist on their other staff being Christians unless they had some kind of role in disseminating information or expressing opinions about the 'ideological guidance' offered by the church or school.

The proposal has caused anxiety among some Christians, and the Christian Institute launched a campaign in June 2000 to try to persuade the British Government not to vote for the present text of the Directive in the Council.[35] Some of my own concerns about the proposal relate to three issues; subsidiarity, human rights, and external competence.

Subsidiarity

Recital 22 of the Commission proposal deals with subsidiarity. However it does not meet the requirements of paragraphs 4 and 5 of the Protocol on Subsidiarity and Proportionality which was agreed as part of the Treaty of Amsterdam and came into force on 1 May 1999. A failure to comply with the Protocol means that the Directive should be struck down by the European Court of Justice if its lawfulness is challenged in that Court within two months of the adoption of the legislation. The problem is that only the Council, Commission and Member States will have standing to bring such a challenge under Article 230 of the EC Treaty and they will not do so if the Member States have voted for the measure by unanimity in the Council. Thus pressure should be brought to bear on the Member States – particularly the United Kingdom – to face up to the subsidiarity dimension now and seek reforms of the Directive in the Council.

An *ex-post facto* legal challenge could only take place if the issue of the validity of the Directive arose in proceedings in a national court and that court decided to refer the issue of validity to the European Court of Justice for a preliminary ruling under Article 234 of the EC Treaty.[36]

Paragraph 4 of the Protocol on Subsidiarity and Proportionality requires that 'the reasons for concluding that a Community objective can be better achieved by the Community must be substantiated by qualitative or, wherever possible, quantitative indicators'. Recital 22 of the draft Directive gives no quantitative indicators and asserts subsidiarity compliance rather than giving qualitative indicators of such compliance. Admittedly the explanatory memorandum goes a little further in paragraph 3.1 but even here the quantitative data relates only to gender discrimination. No clear justification is given for two of the most controversial parts of the Directive – discrimination on grounds of sexual orientation and on grounds of religious belief. In any case it is doubtful whether statements in the explanatory memorandum (which are made by the Commission and cannot be altered by the other legislative institutions in the Community) can be used to justify compliance with the requirements of paragraphs 4 and 5 of the Protocol on Subsidiarity and Proportionality.

If we look at paragraph 5 of the Protocol there is a strong case for saying that the draft Directive intrudes into the normal matters of internal life in Member States and that the 'transnational aspects' are very small due to very few people moving across frontiers to work and being denied jobs on the grounds of their sexual orientation or religious belief. Most cases caught by this Directive will be purely domestic or internal to the country concerned. In such circumstances there is a very strong case for saying that these decisions should be taken as 'closely as possible to the citizen' (Article 1 of the Treaty on European Union). Decisions about the balance between the rights of particular groups in society to preserve their rights to group identity (eg Christians, Jews, Muslims, political parties) and thereby to discriminate against people who want to work for the group but will not accept some or all of the group's core values (eg a male-only leadership or a rejection of the validity of homosexual practice) should be taken much closer to the citizen than in Brussels. This is a matter to be decided in Edinburgh or London where the decision makers can take account of the delicate balancing needed between conflicting rights (eg the right to freedom of religion and belief – Article 9 of the European Convention on Human Rights

(ECHR); the right to freedom of association – Article 11 ECHR; and the right to non-discrimination – Article 14 ECHR, which does not include sexual orientation discrimination). The importance of such balancing is seen in the Human Rights Act 1998 discussed above.

Paragraph 7 of the Protocol on Subsidiarity and Proportionality should also be examined. It says that:

> Community measures should leave as much scope for national decision as possible ... care should be taken to respect well established national arrangements and the organisation and working of Member States' legal systems. Where appropriate and subject to the need for proper enforcement, Community measures should provide Member States with alternative ways to achieve the objectives of the measures.

It would seem that the draft Directive does not leave enough scope for the balancing of conflicting rights and elevates non-discrimination to the highest right of all. This is a kind of liberal fundamentalism which makes it difficult or impossible for a Christian medical practice only to hire Christian doctors, for a Jewish hospice only to hire Jews, for a Muslim society only to appoint heterosexuals to office, etc. Such fundamental value judgements should not be made for the whole of the European Union in Brussels given its remoteness from the full democratic processes and the limited capacity of citizens to effectively influence the outcomes.[37]

Human rights

Elevating the right to non-discrimination above other human rights may be unlawful under Community law. The European Court of Justice can strike down Community legislation on the grounds that it is contrary to fundamental rights. The Court has recognised freedom of religion as a fundamental right in Case 130/75 *Prais* v *Council* [1976] ECR 1589. In order to make the rights to freedom of religion, association and expression meaningful it should be possible for groups of people in society to explicitly set themselves up as offering a service based on a particular set of beliefs and to ensure that the people who work for those groups adhere to the common values which are at the heart of the group. Therefore a Christian medical practice should be able to employ only people that adhere to Christian teachings – including the teaching that homosexual practice is sinful and should be able to exclude non-Christian doctors or Christian doctors that are practising homosexuals. Yet such a Christian medical practice may not be protected by either of the possible exceptions in Article 4 of the Directive. The rights of these Christians to associate as Christians and provide a specialist medical service based on a clear Christian ethos could be removed in Brussels unless the European Court of Justice is careful to give a very broad construction to the exceptions in Article 4 in order to protect rights to association and freedom of religion. If the Member States do not take advantage of these exceptions then the Court of Justice may need to be persuaded to build in some minimal protection for these rights in its interpretation of the Directive or to go further and declare the Directive invalid for not guaranteeing such minimum protection.[38]

External competence

In policy terms one has to question the wisdom of giving the Commission a mixed competence with Member States in external relations in this delicate field of the balance between the right to non-discrimination and the right to allow groups of people to have a distinctive identity which means their focus is based on their religious beliefs and these beliefs conflict with the liberal consensus about non-discrimination on grounds of religion or sexual orientation. The creation of external competence is a by-product of adopting the Directive and should be kept to a minimum by passing only the non-controversial aspects of the Directive. The Commission is not an elected body and has a recent track record of taking on too many things and not accepting responsibility for dealing with them.[39]

CONCLUSION

The Christian community should unite in protecting the liberty of Christians to live their lives in accordance with biblical teaching. The Christian community needs to think long and hard about how it can be salt and light in the world in the context of legislation that goes beyond simply protecting the liberties of Christians to live their lives as Christians. Some Christians will emphasise the need to protect the liberties of others, including those of other faiths and of no faiths and including minority groups like homosexuals. All Christians should respect such a position. Other Christians will want to work with non-Christians to produce 'good legislation' and will use Christian arguments to support their campaign. Such people follow in the footsteps of William Wilberforce and the Seventh Earl of Shaftesbury who helped to bring about the abolition of slavery and improvements in working conditions.[40] All Christians should respect such a position unless the legislation does represent a threat to the freedom of conscience and religion of non-Christians. However, Christians might have legitimate concerns about the appropriate level for decisions to be made about controversial issues, whether it should be in Edinburgh, London or Brussels, and different Christians would take different views on this matter. In relation to the substantive issues a key question is – would we support non-discrimination laws against practising homosexuals provided Christian organisations are allowed to discriminate against such persons or would we oppose all non-discrimination laws on the ground of sexual orientation? We have to accept the fact that Christians will be divided as to the answer to this question and recognise that there is more than one valid Christian perspective on what the law should be.

Notes

1. 'Christian Perspectives on the Law: what makes them distinctive'.
2. In fact the law had already departed from a strict fault system in that in a non-fault situation the 'innocent' spouse could only hold up the divorce for five years.
3. See Lord Mackay of Clashfern, 'Family Law Reform: A personal view' in Beaumont and Wotherspoon (eds), *Christian Perspectives on Law and Relationism* (Carlisle: Paternoster, 2000). First given as a lecture at the Lawyers' Christian Fellowship Conference in Aberdeen in September 1998.
4. See his foreword to Paul Beaumont (ed.), *Christian Perspectives on Law Reform* (Carlisle: Paternoster, 1998).
5. *Christian Perspectives on Law Reform*, op. cit., n. 4; *Christian Perspectives on Human Rights and Legal Philosophy*, op. cit., n. 20; *Christian Perspectives on Law and Relationism*, op. cit., n. 3; *Christian Perspectives on the Limits of Law*, op. cit., n. 19.
6. In June 1999 the Labour Government announced that it would delay indefinitely the bringing into force of the provisions on divorce in the Family Law Act 1996 (Part II). A decision which has been criticised by some family law specialists, eg [1999] *Family Law* 745–7 and 801. The main reason for the Labour Government's decision is probably the extra cost to the exchequer of putting in place mandatory information meetings.
7. Op. cit., n. 3. The key passages are Matthew 19:1–12 and 1 Corinthians 7:10–16.
8. The initial reform was done by the Divorce Reform Act 1969 and replicated in the Matrimonial Causes Act 1973 which repealed the 1969 Act; see s.1 of both Acts for the provision on the ground for divorce being 'that the marriage has broken down irretrievably'.
9. See s.2 of the Divorce Reform Act 1969 and now s.1(2) of the Matrimonial Causes Act 1973. The adultery fact has to be combined with the fact that 'the petitioner finds it intolerable to live with the respondent'; the desertion has to be for a period of two years; and the 'unreasonable behaviour' is a shorthand for the fact 'that the respondent has behaved in such a way that the petitioner cannot reasonably be expected to live with the respondent'.
10. Though fault would have remained relevant in certain circumstances for the splitting of property and for the decisions about custody and access in relation to any children involved.
11. The final time period agreed in the Family Law Act 1996 is a little complicated. There is a nine-month period for reflection and consideration which begins fourteen days after the statement of marital

breakdown is received by the court and that statement can only be given if the party making it has attended an information meeting not less than three months before making the statement (see ss.5–8 of the Act).

12. Op. cit., n. 3.
13. Ibid.
14. Ibid.
15. See s.8 of the 1996 Act.
16. Op. cit., n. 3.
17. Ibid.
18. Ibid.
19. See Julian Rivers, 'Liberal Constitutionalism and Christian Political Thought' in Paul Beaumont (ed.), *Christian Perspectives on the Limits of Law* (Carlisle: Paternoster, 2001).
20. 'Towards a Christian Approach to Religious Liberty' in Paul Beaumont (ed.), *Christian Perspectives on Human Rights and Legal Philosophy* (Carlisle: Paternoster, 1998), pp. 31–72, esp. pp. 59–72.
21. See s.6 of the Human Rights Act 1998 for the definition.
22. Ibid., s.3(1).
23. See Leigh, op. cit., n. 20 at p. 62.
24. S.6(3)(a).
25. Ledingham Chalmers European Law lecture in the University of Aberdeen in May 1999.
26. See Leigh, op. cit., n. 20 at p. 61.
27. Ibid., at pp. 67–9 for the details.
28. Ibid., at pp. 70–1.
29. Art. 136 EC states the objectives as being: 'the promotion of employment, improved living and working conditions, so as to make possible their harmonisation while the improvement is being maintained, proper social protection, dialogue between management and labour, the development of human resources with a view to lasting high employment and the combating of exclusion'.
30. COM (1999) 565 final.
31. Ibid., Art. 1.
32. Ibid., Art. 3.
33. Ibid., Art. 4(1).
34. Ibid., Art. 4(2).
35. The Christian Institute, *European Threat to Religious Freedom* (Newcastle: Christian Institute, 2000).
36. See Stephen Weatherill and Paul Beaumont, *EU Law* (3rd edn, London: Penguin, 1999), chapters 8 and 9.
37. For a thorough critique of the sort of liberal fundamentalism which elevates non-discrimination above religious liberty see Leigh, op. cit., n. 20 at pp. 31–52.
38. See Weatherill and Beaumont, op.cit., n. 36 at pp. 284–90, for a brief discussion of the European Court of Justice's doctrine of fundamental human rights which can be used by that Court to strike down Community legislation which does not conform with those rights.
39. See the Committee of Independent Experts Report of 15 March 1999 noted in Weatherill and Beaumont, op. cit., n. 36 at pp. 1059–64.
40. See Teresa Sutton, 'Christians as Law Reformers in the Nineteenth and Twentieth Centuries', in Paul Beaumont (ed.), *Christian Perspectives on Law Reform* (Carlisle: Paternoster, 1998), pp. 7–24.

THE FUTURE OF THE FAMILY

A Crisis of Commitment

More people than ever are divorcing, bringing up children alone or living as a couple without marrying. So is family life important? Is any action needed to support it? This book tackles these and other questions from a Christian perspective.
Paper/0 86153 157 4/72pp/£4.95

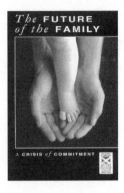

HUMAN GENETICS

A Christian Perspective

Human genetics affects us all. It is changing the way we all look at human life, and understand ourselves. Quite rightly, many people are looking to the Church for guidance and support. This book offers everyone an informed starting point for further reflection from a Christian perspective.
Paper/0 86153 208 2/76pp/£4.95

PRE-CONCEIVED IDEAS

A Christian Perspective of IVF and Embryology

Many people have pre-conceived ideas about fertilisation and embryology. In this book, the Church of Scotland gives a Christian perspective on these complex issues. It also offers helpful advice about the possibilities and problems of starting a family by IVF and other methods.
Paper/0 86153 223 6/96pp/£5.95

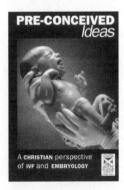

The books are available from
SAINT ANDREW PRESS
Church of Scotland, 121 George Street, Edinburgh EH2 4YN
and from all good bookshops.

BIO-ETHICS FOR THE NEW MILLENNIUM
Lectures Delivered at a Major Conference on Human Genetics
New advances in human genetics are rarely out of the media spotlight. Each development has crucial implications for society as a whole. This book contains nine lectures on the ethical issues of genetics, offering fascinating insights from the scientific, academic and theological viewpoints.
Paper / 0 86153 305 4 / 96pp / £7.95

The packs below are available direct from
The CHURCH of SCOTLAND BOARD of SOCIAL RESPONSIBILITY
Charis House, 47 Milton Road East, Edinburgh EH15 2SR.
(Add £1.00 p&p for each item ordered. Cheques payable to 'Board of Social Responsibility'.)

Social Inclusion
A Study Pack for Churches
A helpful pack for congregations, including useful material and a questionnaire about social inclusion.
£4.00

Marriage PLUS
A Study Pack for Couples
A pack for couples about to get married, or for use by those leading marriage preparation classes.
£4.00